D1199447

HOWARD HUGHES
in Hollywood

HOWARD HUGHES

in Hollywood

by Tony Thomas

Citadel Press   **Secaucus, New Jersey**

Copyright © 1985 by Tony Thomas

All rights reserved. No part of this book
may be reproduced in any form, except by
a newspaper or magazine reviewer who wishes
to quote brief passages in connection
with a review.

Published by Citadel Press
A division of Lyle Stuart Inc.
120 Enterprise Ave., Secaucus, N.J. 07094
In Canada: Musson Book Company
A division of General Publishing Co. Limited.
Don Mills, Ontario

Queries regarding rights and permissions should be
addressed to: Lyle Stuart, 120 Enterprise Avenue,
Secaucus, N.J. 07094

Manufactured in the United States of America

Library of Congress Cataloging in Publication Data

Thomas, Tony, 1927-
    Howard Hughes in Hollywood.

    Includes index.
    1. Hughes, Howard, 1905-1976.   I. Title.
PN1998.A3H737   1985   791.43′0232′0924   85-6686

ISBN 0-8065-0970-8 (paperback)
ISBN 0-8065-0976-7 (hardcover)

Acknowledgments

Most of the research into the films of Howard Hughes was done at the library of The Academy of Motion Picture Arts and Sciences, for which I am indebted to Linda Mehr and her staff. In writing the chapter on *Hell's Angels* I was helped by the research already done on that film by Rudy Behlmer. For helping me delve into Hughes memorabilia, particularly in regard to photographs, I am grateful to Richard Gano, Sr., Richard Gano, Jr., and Bill M. Winberg. Other photos came through the assistance of Eddie Brandt's *Saturday Matinee* (North Hollywood) and Collectors Book Shop (Hollywood). Without this help the book would not have been possible.

Tony Thomas

Contents

HOWARD HUGHES
in Hollywood

1

Who Was Howard Hughes?

During the first five days of April, 1976, a man lay dying in a penthouse atop the posh Acapulco Princess Hotel in Acapulco, Mexico. The view from that twentieth floor was spectacular, but it was a view he never saw because the penthouse was continuously draped and darkened, as was almost every hotel suite he had occupied in the final decade of his life. He was seventy, but it would have been impossible for anyone to estimate his age because he was now a decayed, emaciated wreck. He had shriveled during long years of self-imposed illness, but his body was still six feet in length. It was, however, a mere ninety-three pounds in weight. He looked like one of those pitiful living corpses found in Nazi concentration camps in April of 1945.

He could hardly have been in worse condition had he been a derelict lying in a back alley of a forgotten slum, waiting for death to end it all. As a derelict he might have fared better, had someone picked him up and carted him off to a hospital for treatment. But this man happened to be a billionaire with an imposing name. He was by nature a totally self-willed human being and due to his wealth and the power that it commanded he was able to refuse help, to refuse to see a doctor or go to a hospital, or even to eat and drink properly. The team of aides, a half-dozen of them, found him impossible to tend—until that final day when he lapsed into unconsciousness and could no longer tell them what not to do.

Hughes at the premiere of his first hit film, *Two Arabian Knights*, in 1927.

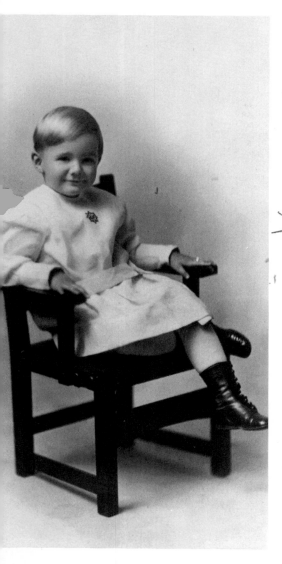

Howard Hughes at three.

This was how the life of the incredible Howard Hughes ended. When an aide called the high command at the Hughes Aircraft Company in Los Angeles, arrangements were immediately made to fly him to Houston, Texas, the city in which Hughes was born on December 24, 1905. His body showed barely any signs of life when he was carried from the hotel and placed aboard a small jet airplane, and he was dead by the time it landed in Houston. His heart, after years of abuse, finally gave out. There was at least a little poetic justice in the death—Howard Hughes had died in an airplane in flight, and it was in the air, and only in the air, that he felt at home.

According to the astrologers, Capricorns are hard working, practical, constructive people but sometimes hampered by the tendency to worry and to find the hard way of doing things. They are not happy-go-lucky. If this is true, then Hughes stands as an affirmation of astrology. He was a man who not only did things the hard way but who never sought advice and who certainly never heeded any. Hughes was entirely his own man and no yardstick of conventional human behavior can be applied to him. He was willful in the extreme, and he was a mass of contradictions. Hughes was both timid and bold, he was chronically shy and hated even to have his photo taken but he was keenly concerned about his name and public image.

Had he ever agreed to appear on the television program *To Tell the Truth*—and the likelihood of such a withdrawn man doing anything so public is less than remote—then how would he have appeared when asked, "Will the real Howard Hughes please stand up"? Who would have stood there? Would it have been Howard Hughes the industrialist? Hughes the aviator—the man who designed, built and raced airplanes? Would it have been the man who once gained a conspicuous reputation as an elusive bachelor and seemed to have dated half the famous actresses of Hollywood? Would it have been Hughes the film maker? or would it have been the man who evolved into a bizarre recluse? If nothing else, the man who stood there would have had to have been regarded as unique because there was nothing in his life and behavior that could be compared with any other man's.

There are lines of consistency in all our lives. With Hughes the most consistent line was one of loneliness, of isolation and the lack of ability to relate closely to other people. He was an only child and both parents had strong, commanding personalities. His father, Howard Robard Hughes, was trained as a lawyer but his passion lay in mining and finding out what was under the surface of the earth. Eventually he found oil under the surface of Texas, but what gave shape to his ambitions was finding a Dallas beauty named Allene Gano, who belonged to a prominent and influential Texas family.

As an oilman, Hughes, like all the others, was constantly frustrated by inadequate drilling equipment, especially the lack of a drill that could pierce solid rock and get to the massive amounts of oil that the geologists had advised lay beneath the rock strata of Texas. Hughes was something of an inventor, or at least a tinkerer, and after much tinkering he devised a conical drill bit with 162 cutting edges, plus a means of lubricating it as it dug into rock. When it proved successful, Hughes patented it and set up a factory in Houston. He had the foresight not to sell the drill bits but to lease them, and within a few years Hughes's invention was being used in three-quarters of the oil drilling activity throughout the world. Many years later Howard Hughes, Junior, was asked by a journalist if the Hughes Tool Company held a monopoly on this operation. Replied Hughes: "No, people who want to drill for oil and not use the Hughes bit can always use a pick and shovel."

Howard Hughes was barely three years of age when his father made the breakthrough from which an empire would grow. By that age he was already showing signs of mechanical aptitude, playing with wires and scraps of metal to build little things. He also at this age knew how to operate a box camera and gained obvious pleasure at looking at things through the lens. As a schoolboy he showed no signs of unusual intelligence, except in mathematics. He spent a lot of time playing by himself, and in school he was the kind of child who made himself as inconspicuous as possible.

With success, Howard Hughes senior became more and more social. Gregarious and charming by nature, and with a wife whose natural habitat was high society, he freely spent the large amounts of money that flowed into Hughes Tool Company. The Hugheses enjoyed life as their son quietly stood in the background, greatly attached to his devoted mother and greatly in awe of his personable father. Those who came to know the son years later claim that despite acquiring much greater fame and fortune, Howard Hughes never considered himself the equal of his father.

At the age of fourteen Howard was enrolled in the Fessenden School in West Newton, Massachusetts. He did fairly well at his studies, but with puberty it was still the mechanical side of his nature that prevailed and not the intellectual. During a vacation period at home his mother denied him a motorcycle, believing it to be unsafe. Howard then turned his bicycle into a motorized vehicle by using parts from a car self-starter and batteries. On another occasion when his father had promised him he could have his choice of present, the boy chose a ride in a flying boat he had spotted moored on a river. With this ride Howard Hughes discovered the joy of aviation, and that joy quickly became an obsession. It was perhaps the first clear indication of a nature that would gradually become completely obsessive-compulsive.

The drilling bit invented and patented by Hughes senior had a profound bearing upon the American oil industry. It not only helped open up the vast oilfields of southwest Texas, but it was responsible for the development of the oil deposits of southern California, which fact had a profound bearing upon the future of Hughes junior. Senior opened a branch of his tool company in Los Angeles and began to spend more and more of his time in California. In order to have their son nearer, the Hugheses enrolled him in September of 1921 at the Thatcher School in Ojai, twenty-five miles east of Santa Barbara, California. Howard

Twelve-year-old Howard Hughes with his mother at the Houston Country Club, already intent upon being a great golfer.

13

The enterprising 14-year-old Howard Hughes.

appeared to like the school, although he was still shy and retiring and apparently uninterested or incapable of developing close friends. In the privacy he seemed to enjoy he taught himself to play the saxophone, and he tinkered with machinery.

His parents became involved in Los Angeles society, especially with the Hollywood strata. The senior Hughes's brother, Rupert, was a well-established screen writer and it was through him that Howard and his parents met film celebrities and visited studios. Rupert Hughes had been a popular novelist before selling his first screenplay in 1916. Samuel Goldwyn put him under contract and he soon became one of the industry's top scenarists. By 1922 he was also directing and earning a large income, quite a lot of which was spent enjoying life. He became noted for his Sunday parties, which became a weekly gathering of the Hollywood elite and at which his brother, his sister-in-law and his

14

nephew were able to meet almost anyone involved in the picture business.

During the spring term of 1922, the easygoing life of young Howard Hughes received a severe punch. On March 29 his beautiful, thirty-nine-year-old mother entered the Baptist Hospital in Houston for minor surgery on her uterus, from which she expected to leave the hospital in a matter of hours. She never recovered from the anesthetic. Her completely sudden and unexpected death shattered her husband, who could not bring himself to tell his son. That job fell to Uncle Rupert. What affect it had upon Howard was hard to immediately gauge because it was not his nature to show emotion. The long-range effect is easy to assume—that of a withdrawn and lonely boy strongly attached to his mother—but how it would affect his future relationships with women is best left to professional psychiatric interpretation.

Hughes senior had set up his tool company with excellent management and there was little need for him to be in Houston, which he now avoided as much as possible because of its reminders of his wife, over whom he obviously grieved. Probably because of that grief, he took Howard out of the Thatcher School and brought him to live at a house he had bought in Pasadena. The boy was placed in the California Institute of Technology in that city, which required a heavy bribe because he had no high school diploma. Hughes senior had made an arrangement with his sister-in-law Annette to live with them for one year to look after Howard. At the end of that year she refused to extend the agreement because she wanted to return to Houston to get married, which she did, and the elder Hughes decided also to return in order to take a greater command of his flourishing business.

Despite being gifted with mechanical skills, which included being able to build and operate a ham radio station, young Howard showed no clear ambitions. In September of 1923 he began his college life at the Rice Institute in Houston. All seemed well—but another anvil of fate was about to drop on Howard Robard Hughes, Jr.

On the afternoon of January 14, 1924, Hughes senior held a meeting with his sales manager. Suddenly Hughes was struck with a convulsion; he staggered and then fell to the floor, dead from a heart attack. His death was as brutally ironic as that of his wife, since neither had shown any signs of ill health. Both were lively, outgoing and vital, and both stepped from that condition into death.

At his funeral Hughes was rightly eulogized as the man who had revolutionized the American oil industry and praised as a fine and admirable man. No one considered him finer or more admirable than his son. The internal effects of the loss are easy to guage. Coming less than two years after the loss of his mother, the death of the father could only have profoundly affected the son. As an introvert he kept much of this to himself, but there were some obvious manifestations, most of them pertaining to his health. The eighteen-year-old became a hypochondriac, fearful of early death and paranoid about germs. And it was a phobia that grew and grew.

Howard Hughes with his bride Ella at a costume ball in Houston in 1925.

15

Hughes with Bette Davis at the
Tailwaggers Dinner Dance in Hollywood
on the evening of August 13, 1938. Davis
was but one of his many movie star
dates.

The loss of his father had another obvious effect on the son. He did not, as some had supposed for such a withdrawn personality, wither and drift. The death revealed a strength of character that almost no one had expected. Hughes accepted the fact that he was no longer protected by a powerful parent, and he was instantly aware of what he had inherited. The Hughes assets at this time were assessed at well over one million dollars, the major one being the Hughes Tool Company. Hughes senior had left fifty percent of his assets to his wife but with her death they passed to the son, who had been given twenty-five percent. The remaining twenty-five percent was distributed among relatives.

Howard Hughes suddenly showed the independence, the willfullness and the refusal to be swayed by advice that marked him for the remainder of his life. He was not content to be a seventy-five-percent owner and manager of the Hughes Tool Company—he wanted it all. His first step was to leave Rice Institute, since he had no interest in further education, and his next step was to give himself a vacation in Europe. On his return he moved into his father's office and devoted his time to learning how to run a company that was steadily making money. He also hired lawyers. He was keenly aware of his father's advice that a businessman does best if he has no partners, and young Howard Hughes did not want his uncle and his grandparents as partners.

Later Hughes explained: "The thing I knew was that I would never be able to get along with my relations and that's why I was determined to buy them out and go it alone." It took a lot of persuasion to get his way, but four months after the death of Hughes senior the grandparents and Uncle Rupert settled for $325,000. It was bitterly agreed upon and caused a permanent rift with his relations, but it was a price the eighteen-year-old was prepared to pay, both financially and emotionally. He was now fully in command of Hughes Tool Company, and he had learned early in the game that in order to take command it is necessary to be tough with people. It was an attitude from which he never wavered.

In assuming his inheritance, Hughes had also assumed a big problem: According to Texas law he was a minor and could not enter into contracts until he was twenty-one. By rights he should also be provided with a guardian. However, with the aid of his lawyers he discovered a statutory provision of the Texas Legal Code that would allow a minor to plead his case in court and obtain a declaration of competency should he so convince a judge. The application could not be made until his nineteenth birthday, December 24, 1924. Two days later he appeared in Probate Court and performed in a manner that led Judge Walter Montieth to declare Howard Hughes to be legally of full age and free of the disabilities of being a minor. From then and for the rest of his life Hughes did as he wished.

Hughes Senior had never been greatly interested in the mechanics of running the Hughes Tool Company, beyond making certain that it was well staffed and capable of virtually running itself. His son soon came to the same decision. He, too, had little liking for the administrative side of

17

operating a factory and, perhaps instinctively, he decided it would be better to stay away from it. He knew it to be the mainspring of his wealth, but he had another reason—he wanted it to be a memorial in continuum to his father.

In his twentieth year Hughes had no defined ambition or any qualifications other than a mechanical aptitude. He spent time tinkering with building a new kind of steam-driven automobile, but he finally decided to take a chance on being a film maker in Hollywood. He had long been fascinated by his visits to the studios and by the way movies were made. But he was at this time also fascinated by a girl in Houston. Her name was Ella Rice, a vivacious beauty two years his senior and as much an extrovert as he was an introvert.

Ella Rice was not a likely prospect to become Mrs. Howard Hughes. She belonged among the top level of Houston society—indeed, she was a member of the family after which Rice Institute was named—and she was courted by squads of eager young gentlemen. Hughes had admired her from afar for years, but he had made no more impression upon her than he had on the other girls he had bashfully gazed upon. He had now reached his full height of six feet three inches and it had done nothing to lessen the awkwardness he had felt all through his teenage years. He felt especially awkward in high society, caring nothing for that kind of lifestyle. On the other hand he had also reached a growth of character, the main facet of which was doggedness. The pattern had begun to emerge—whatever Howard wanted Howard got. He got Ella Rice as his wife. They were married on a hot and humid first of June, 1925, in the garden of Ella's sister Libby's home, and the wedding was attended by hordes of Houston's upper crust. It was the event of the season.

In marrying Ella Rice, Hughes had followed his father's example— he had married a beautiful Texas aristocrat—although it may have been a decision he arrived at subconsciously. Despite his wealth he was virtually an orphan, estranged from most of his relatives and a man with few close friends. In point of fact, the only man he ever referred to as a close friend was Dudley Sharp, the son of one of his father's colleagues. He was clearly a man in need of love, although there is little evidence that he was capable of loving. Hughes never discussed his personal life, and both of the women he married and divorced refrained from comment.

It is a fair assumption that nineteen-year-old Howard Hughes needed someone in his life, especially since he wanted to leave Houston and start a new chapter of that life elsewhere. He had been a loner from the start, and sadly that is what he would always be, but loners are not always that way by choice. No doubt Hughes felt he had ceased to be a loner in that summer of 1925 as he was about to set out for California with a beautiful wife.

Two days before getting married, Hughes put his name to a will. The first stipulation was that his friend Dudley Sharp should get ten thousand dollars. This was followed by higher amounts to relatives on his mother's side, but none to those who had benefitted in his father's will, those whom Hughes junior had bought out. There were stipends for

Hughes in 1927 with Carl Laemmle, the owner of Universal Studios.

a half-dozen executives in Hughes Tool Company and, as could be expected, a generous consideration of his bride-to-be. Ella would receive half a million dollars in securities. However, the most extensively written part of the will involved a corporation to be set up and titled Howard R. Hughes Medical Research Laboratories. Its funds were specified for scientific research into ways of discovering and developing cures for the diseases that plague humankind. The young hypochondriac had made his wishes known, and that regard for medical research remained a passion with him. In view of this constant interest it becomes incomprehensible that he would develop such a shocking disregard for his own health in his last years and totally ignore the benefits he had helped to sponsor. It is, of course, all part of the mystery and the set of epic contradictions that made up Howard Hughes.

However, in that summer of 1925 he was a happy man. He enjoyed showing off Ella to his maternal relatives in Dallas, and his adoring bride looked on with pleasure as Howard indulged himself in the one sport he loved—golf. He resolved to become one of the greatest golfers in the world. He had to settle for becoming merely a very good one, finding, as have many others, that it is a game that eludes mastery no matter how great the determination. There are exceptions, but he was not one of them.

Howard and Ella Hughes left Houston in September and took the train for Los Angeles. He had convinced her of his prospects in becoming a film producer, and since money was not a worry in their lives, she had no reason to doubt him. Besides, he had put his affairs in order—he had made a will. Apparently, and unfortunately, it seems to have been the only will to which Howard Hughes put his signature, something that created utter chaos when he died.

19

Ralph Graves, the star-director of the
never released *Swell Hogan*.

One Miss, Four Hits

The Hollywood in which Howard and Ella Hughes took up residence in the fall of 1925 was a thriving, highly productive beehive of an industry-town. A generation earlier it had been a sleepy, barely noticeable suburb of Los Angeles. Now it was not simply the capital of the American film industry, it was the foremost place in the world for the production of motion pictures. It was also, as it still largely is, a cultural island populated by talented but vain, self-centered people, drawn not only from every walk of life but from almost every part of the world. In short, it was a mecca, but a mecca unlike any ever before known. It may have seemed glamorous—indeed, glamor was its primary product—but underneath the flashy surface of Hollywood was a vast amount of tough dealing and not a little despair.

In the movie business it is said that the only job that needs no qualifications is that of producer; all it needs is enough money to put up a sign on a door and start hiring people. Like so many things said in Hollywood, the remark is duplicitous, since most of those who mouth it are quite willing to line up and be hired. When Hughes made his foray into the picture business there was little reason for people to regard him as other than "the sucker with the dough." There had been lots of that kind; they came and they went.

In appearance, Hughes could hardly avoid being taken lightly. He was a mere twenty-year-old from Houston, the product of a monied

Everybody's Acting, with Gloria Heller and Philo McCullough.

Henry Walthall, Betty Bronson and
Lawrence Gray in *Everybody's Acting*.

background, and he was shy, gangling and quiet. It took a little while for
Hollywood to discover what his relatives in Houston had already
observed—that behind the rather naïve façade was a young man with a
spine of steel, and that it was impossible to advise him. To tell him that
something could not or should not be done was a waste of time, because
he would prove everybody wrong and do it.

In November of 1925 Hughes took the first step toward being a
successful businessman by hiring an accountant named Noah Dietrich.
Dietrich soon became more than the man who kept the books; he was a
rather gruff, tough character who had once been a racing driver, and he
had a cool, perceptive understanding of finance. He was soon Hughes's
financial adviser and over the years he would become one of the
strongest officers in the Hughes empire. It was a relationship that lasted
for more than thirty-one years, until May of 1957 when Dietrich strongly
advised Hughes to take steps he did not want to take and he was fired.
The two men never saw or spoke to each other again. However, in late
1925 Howard Hughes badly needed someone like Noah Dietrich to ward
off the Hollywood wolves.

The first man to take advantage of Hughes was an actor named
Ralph Graves, although in Hughes's defense it must be said that Hughes
senior had made it difficult for junior to avoid the trap into which he
was about to fall. Graves was from Houston and was much admired by
Hughes senior, who at one point put him on the tool company payroll
when Graves was between jobs as an actor. Senior made known his
admiration to his son and suggested that if he ever went to Hollywood to
make pictures, and it seemed he might, he should look out for Ralph

William Boyd and Louis Wolheim in *Two Arabian Knights.*

Graves, who was not only a good talent but a nice man.

Graves approached young Hughes and told him he had acquired a story and that he had put it into script form, and, to use the words that have echoed through the Hollywood hills for decades, "It'll make a hell of a movie." It was called *Swell Hogan* and it was about a good-hearted Bowery derelict who is forever doing good turns, such as helping orphans. As an actor, Graves had little difficulty persuading Hughes that it was a good script. Hughes said he would like to do it but that he would need a lot of help in putting a production together since he knew little about the mechanics of picture making. Graves assured him that this was not a problem, since he would not only play the role of Hogan but would direct it and act as production supervisor. This seemed reasonable in view of Graves's film experience; after all, he had been acting in movies since 1918.

The budget for *Swell Hogan* was set at $40,000, which in 1926 was average for a program picture and was not a sum to faze Hughes. By the time the film was completed the budget had doubled. Whether intentionally or not, the star-director took his time about getting his performance on camera and the young producer hired a far larger crew than was necessary to make such a modest movie. No one was about to tell him otherwise; he was "the sucker with the money." But Hughes was no sucker when he set down to look at the completed film. It was rubbish. It had no structure, no plot, no tension and the acting was ludicrous. Hughes ordered the film to be placed in a vault, from which it never emerged.

The fact that *Swell Hogan* was never shown did no harm to Ralph

23

Graves. He was not the only actor to make an unreleased picture, and he knew Hughes was not likely to make any commotion about it. Graves continued his career and acted in movies until 1939. But the episode had been a valuable lesson for Hughes, who had indeed found out about the mechanics of picture making and the need to make a careful study of talent before hiring it. No aspect of the business now escaped Hughes. He even took cameras and projectors apart and put them back together in order to find out how the equipment worked.

Making a dud did not halt Hughes's resolve to become a film maker. He sought out scripts, and settled on one titled *Everybody's Acting*, the plot of which was written by Marshall Neilan. Neilan had also been a friend of Hughes senior, but junior had no qualms about hiring him because Neilan had a solid reputation as a director, having directed a couple of dozen films since 1919. With Neilan under contract Hughes was able to make a distribution deal with Paramount, then under the command of the respected Adolph Zukor and Jesse Lasky. Although the plot of the film had been devised by Neilan, he advised Hughes to hire Benjamin Glazer to turn it into a screenplay, and George Marion, Jr., to supply the titles to this silent comedy. Both men were established talents and Hughes stood quietly on the sidelines as they and the others did their work. In years to come he would be notorious for interfering, but at this stage he wisely kept his distance.

Everybody's Acting was a success and brought Hughes enough profit to cover his losses on *Swell Hogan*. The public found it amusing and the critics said that it was mostly a piece of well-made fluff, an opinion which its producer was happy to accept. Neilan's lightweight plot was about a group of five actors who adopt an orphaned baby girl, who grows into a handsome young lady (Betty Bronson). They bring her up in the atmosphere of the theatre and teach her everything they can about the business. She falls in love with a young taxi driver (Lawrence Gray) who wants to be a novelist but who is actually the son of a wealthy, domineering society matron (Louise Dresser). The mother is appalled by the idea of her son's marrying a common actress. The five foster fathers then devise a scheme to impress the stuffy old lady: They hire a home and act as the girl's father and her staff. The matron is pleased, but the girl decides she cannot win her man with such deceit and confesses it all. The young man is sent to a job in the Far East by his angry mother, but the foster fathers manage to get their girl on the same ship. Finally the mater recognizes defeat and sends her blessings. Edited down to a crisp sixty-five minutes, *Everybody's Acting* served precisely the purpose for which it was made. For Paramount it was simply product, but for Hughes it was the foot in the door.

In their first few months in Hollywood, Howard and Ella lived at the Ambassador Hotel on Wilshire Boulevard in Los Angeles, but with the success of *Everybody's Acting* they moved to a house on Muirfield Road in Hancock Park, about a mile or so west of the hotel. Hancock Park continues to be one of the classier areas of Los Angeles and is today noted as the section in which the city's diplomatic and consular corps

24

Two Arabian Knights, with William Boyd and Mary Astor.

Two Arabian Knights: Louis Wolheim, William Boyd and Michael Vavitch as the Emir of Jaffa.

The Mating Call, with Thomas Meighan, Evelyn Brent and Alan Roscoe.

Renée Adorée, Thomas Meighan and Evelyn Brent in *The Mating Call*.

26

choose to reside. In the late Twenties, however, it was a posh region for movie wealth, and for Hughes it had the added attraction of backing onto the fairways of the Wilshire Country Club, where he almost daily indulged his passionate affair with golf. What was far less passionate was his marriage. Ella Hughes not only found herself a golf widow but a wife playing second fiddle to her husband's business interests. She also found herself a misfit in the so-called Hollywood society, which to her was not society but a band of *nouveaux riches* who could discuss only one topic—movies. Her friends mostly lived in Pasadena, a city on the eastern boundaries of Los Angeles which still maintains a disdainful regard for Hollywood and its people.

Having no regard for society of any kind in any city, Howard Hughes paid scant attention to his wife's dilemma. With the help of Noah Dietrich he set up his own motion picture company. Rather than create a new company, he was advised by Dietrich to add a subsidiary to one of his corporations, the Caddo Rock Drill Bit Company of Louisiana, allowing it to produce films as well as lease drilling equipment. Hughes opened offices in the Taft Building on Hollywood Boulevard and started to look for other film properties. *Everybody's Acting* was released in November of 1926, a little more than a year after Hughes had set foot in Hollywood. In that period he had had a miss and a hit and he had just about broken even. It may not have been a spectacular year, but it was above average for any fledgling movie producer.

Fate now brought Hughes together with a remarkable man, and it turned out to be a fortuitous meeting for both of them. Lewis Milestone was born in the Ukraine and came to America as a teenager just before the First World War. He served in the war in the U.S. Army Signal Corps and then headed for California to find any kind of work in the film business. He found a job as a cutter and within two years was an assistant director, a job that revealed his talent for writing story treatments. In 1925 Warners gave Milestone his first job as a director, making *Seven Sinners* with comedienne Marie Prevost, which the studio liked so much that they immediately assigned him to Prevost's next picture, *The Caveman*. The reviews made it obvious that Hollywood had discovered a man with a distinct talent for directing movies.

Lewis Milestone was a feisty, self-willed man and quick to temper. He disagreed with Warners over his next assignment and stormed out of the studio. Refusing to come back to work, he was threatened with the familiar cry, "You'll never work in this town again," a cry that unfortunately had some weight in an industry as tightly structured as Hollywood, where studio chieftains tended to close ranks on mutual issues even though they may have been business rivals. It was, however, a cry that meant nothing to Howard Hughes, who never closed ranks with anyone or abided by any set of standards. Through an intermediary he arranged a meeting with Milestone and asked him if he would be interested in directing an adventure comedy about the First World War called *Two Arabian Knights*.

Two Arabian Knights, Caddo's first production, was clearly inspired

27

The Mating Call: Thomas Meighan and Renée Adorée.

by the success of *What Price Glory?*, which Raoul Walsh had recently directed with Edmund Lowe and Victor McLaglen as the endlessly battling Sergeant Flagg and Captain Quirt. Hughes had hired James T. O'Donohue and Wallace Smith to turn the short story by Donald McGibney into a screenplay, with the ever busy George Marion, Jr., supplying the titles. O'Donohue had been one of the scenarists on *What Price Glory?* so there could hardly be any doubt in Hughes's mind as to what kind of picture he was after. But he made it plain to Milestone that he wanted a different approach to the material. Whatever doubts Milestone might have had were dispelled when Hughes outlined his budget at half a million dollars and that he intended to hire the esteemed William Cameron Menzies as his art director, together with two fine cameramen, Tony Gaudio and Joseph August.

The protagonists of *Two Arabian Knights* are a pair of American soldiers—Private W. Daingerfield Phelps and Sergeant Peter McGaffney—who, like Flagg and Quirt, scrap with each other whenever they are not scrapping with the common foe. To play them Hughes and Milestone chose William Boyd and Louis Wolheim. Boyd, who would later make a fortune playing Hopalong Cassidy, had been in films since 1919 and so had German-born Wolheim. One was charming and handsome and the other was almost poetically ugly. They were perfect for this film, and its success sparked both careers. Hughes would use them again and Milestone would have notable success with Wolheim as one of the stars of his *All Quiet on the Western Front.* Tragically that success led nowhere for Wolheim, because he died suddenly in 1931, not long after the film was released.

28

The Racket: Police captain Thomas Meighan warns reporters Richard "Skeets" Gallagher and Lee Moran to "Keep sober." Walter Long is the sergeant.

Two Arabian Knights was knockabout comedy, but Milestone's direction kept it taut and mobile and Hughes's money allowed for superior production values. The story begins in the trenches as the two soldiers take time out from their own bickerings to face the enemy. They are taken prisoner by the Germans and thereafter make continual attempts to escape. They are successful when they disguise themselves as Arabs and, as such, book passage on a ship sailing for Jaffa. On board is a beautiful Arabian girl named Mirza (Mary Astor), and the battling buddies vie for her attention. In Jaffa someone informs her fiancé of her relationship with the Americans, and her father, who turns out to be the emir, plans to imprison them. The American consul brings pressure to bear in their favor and the emir gives them knighthoods in order that Phelps may formally duel with the fiancé. They manage to avoid this and end up escaping Palestine and taking Mirza with them.

Despite its improbable plot, *Two Arabian Knights* pleased not only the public but the critics. Reviewing it for *The New York Times*, Mordaunt Hall wrote, "If common sense direction, intelligent acting with genial humor have succeeded in this instance, then it should inspire other producers to abandon the old bag of tricks and make fun without using the china closet, the kitchen or the chimney." In short, it was a winner.

The success of the film was accented on the evening of May 16, 1929, when the first Academy Awards were held, staged in the Blossom Room of the Hollywood Roosevelt Hotel. The Academy of Motion Picture Arts and Sciences had been created two years previously and the first celebration covered films released in 1927 and 1928. *Two Arabian Knights* was released in October of 1927 and Lewis Milestone found

29

himself nominated at best director of a comedy, along with Charles Chaplin for *The Circus* and Ted Wilde for *Speedy*. The winner was Milestone, who became one of the first two directors to receive Oscars. The other, that same evening, was Frank Borzage, who won for *Seventh Heaven* in the category of dramatic direction. It was the only time the Academy made two categories for direction; thereafter it became a single category, no matter the kind of film.

Howard Hughes, of course, had every reason to be pleased with himself. Until that evening he was still regarded as a rich kid playing around at making movies. Now, having pulled in an Oscar with only his third picture, the Hollywood community had to concede that this strange young man was at least serious about the business. In those first two years Hughes was looked upon as someone who would get his fingers burned and then go back to Texas. All the advice was negative, especially that from his family. His greatly successful Uncle Rupert, with whom he was barely on speaking terms, told him that in trying to be a film producer he was bound to fail and lose a great amount of money. According to Lewis Milestone, Hughes once confessed to him that he was actually thinking of giving up after the miserable experience with *Swell Hogan*, but that it was the advice of Rupert and the others that changed his mind. He told Milestone, "My family made it a challenge. I had to prove me right and them wrong."

Hughes had kept his promise to Milestone not to meddle with production, but that did not stop him from being on hand every hour that *Two Arabian Knights* was being made, or staying long after everyone had left so that he could examine equipment. By now he had already acquired a reputation as being unlike anybody else in the picture business, this quiet, lanky young fellow with a strange presence about him. At first meeting he may have seemed easygoing, but as soon as anyone talked business with him it was quickly apparent that he was anything but. He seemed, they said, kind of peculiar.

The first evidence of Hughes's peculiar nature in Hollywood came just after he had made *Swell Hogan* at the General Service Studios in Hollywood. His contract with that studio specified, as per common practice, that whatever sets he had built for his film could be left there and become studio property unless the producer paid to have them removed or destroyed. Hughes thought nothing about this until he heard that Harry Cohn, then an independent producer, had moved a production into General and intended to utilize some of the *Swell Hogan* sets. Hughes then spent $2500 to have the sets destroyed. Years later when Cohn became the powerful head of Columbia Pictures he was still regarded by Hughes as a vulture.

Lewis Milestone had an uneasy experience with Hughes after *Two Arabian Knights* had been completed. Under the terms of his contract Milestone had total command of the editing of the film. Shortly after he had left for a vacation at Lake Arrowhead, an hour or so by car from Los Angeles, Milestone received a telephone call from a friend who warned him that Hughes was at the studio and that he was cutting up the film.

Milestone immediately drove to the studio, where he found Hughes in an editing room with multiple strips of film all around him and viewing them on the editing machine. Milestone angrily wanted to know what was going on. Apparently he was so furious that the calm Hughes found it impossible to talk in the editing room and finally convinced him to go for a ride in his car. Milestone's anger gradually turned to fear as Hughes sped along the roadways and onto the coast highway at close to one hundred miles an hour. Milestone asked Hughes to pull over to the side of the road. Having had his temper cooled by the ride Milestone was now ready for an explanation. Hughes, still quiet and calm, simply told him that all he was doing was trying to understand how Milestone had edited the picture, and that the best way to do that was take it apart shot by shot. The final print of the film was already in the hands of the distributor. Hughes had made himself a copy in order to cut it up. Recalled Milestone, "Hollywood was Howard's classroom. He was learning about movies. He was the type of person who could never accept anything as the truth unless he had learned it or experienced it personally for himself. He would not take anyone's word. He had to do it, then store it away in that genius mind of his."

Sensing that *Two Arabian Knights* would he a hit, Hughes began preliminary production on *Hell's Angels*, starting in October of 1927. It was a Howard Hughes dream project. Not only was he fascinated by aviation, but he was an admirer of the fighter pilots of the First World War. He shared the general opinion that they were the last cavalier-warriors, but he obviously felt more intensely about it than most people. He probably regarded himself as an aerial cavalier and to that end he took several courses in flying, although never telling any of the instructors that he had studied flying with anybody else. In this manner he hoped to pick up as much knowledge as possible and not have any of the instructors assume he knew anything. With subjects in which he was interested, Hughes was the ultimate student.

Hughes received his final papers as a qualified pilot on January 7, 1928. By that time he had already begun to film the aviation sequences of *Hell's Angels* and as a pilot he would also be involved in those sequences. When not actually making the picture, which gradually came to involve almost every waking hour, he flew his own little plane, a Waco, for fun. Neither activity pleased Mrs. Hughes. With each passing month of their life together she seemed to see less and less of him. Setting dates or making social arrangements meant nothing. Hughes never wore a watch and appeared to have no regard for time, a characteristic that would worsen with the years. Ella, who loathed what she referred to as "the Hollywood crowd," found 1928 impossible. Now that he was a pilot and seemingly obsessed with the making of *Hell's Angels*, he became a virtual absentee husband. On October 1 she left for Houston, never to return. A year later her uncontested divorce became final.

Before *Hell's Angels* reached the screen in June of 1930, the public would see two more of Hughes's Caddo productions. The first, *The Racket*, released in the summer of 1928, was a swiftly paced account of

Barry Norton and Thomas Meighan in *The Racket*.

The Racket: Lee Moran is the tripped reporter, Thomas Meighan is the cautioning captain and Louis Wolheim is the protesting onlooker.

crime in gangster-plagued New York, with the firm hand of Lewis Milestone in control. Bartlett Cormack, whose play of the same name had been a hit on Broadway, was hired by Hughes to adapt it for the screen, and Harry Behn and Del Andrews were assigned as the actual scenarists. Hughes also hired two of the men who had helped make a hit of *Two Arabian Knights*, cameraman Tony Gaudio and actor Louis Wolheim, who played the primary villian, a bootleg racketeer named Nick Scarsi.

For the hero, Hughes chose Thomas Meighan, who had been a top leading man all through the Twenties. Meighan, as Captain McQuigg, appears in *The Racket* as the dedicated cop who is determined to put an end to Scarsi. The racketeer has powerful political connections, strong enough to have McQuigg transferred to another and much more peaceful precinct. Scarsi's affairs are complicated by a kid brother (George Stone) who falls in love with a nightclub singer (Marie Prevost), who happens to hate Scarsi. Getting nowhere with the girl, the brother drives angrily away and becomes involved in a hit-and-run accident, killing a man. Scarsi attempts to get his brother out of jail and succeeds, but the escape has been prearranged so that McQuigg can go after Scarsi. The racketeer's career ends in a chase and a fatal shoot-out.

The Racket, despite the many other gangster movies then on the market, fared well with the critics. Milestone's dramatic lighting, his tracking shots and his editing came in for praise. *Variety* made the point that a successful film needs a good story to tell and a director alive to its possibilities, "It grips your interest from the first shot to the last, and never drags for a second." Howard Hughes had another winner.

32

The next Caddo picture, *The Mating Call*, followed *The Racket* by only three months and again Thomas Meighan was the star. This time Hughes chose as his director James Cruze, a man with a high reputation since his success with *The Covered Wagon* in 1923. Walter Woods adapted Rex Beach's novel into a film script and Herman J. Mankiewicz supplied the titles. Like most of the major films in the last years of the silent movies, *The Mating Call* had a musical score. It was written by David Mendoza and William Axt, who were riding high with three hits, *The Big Parade* (1925), *Ben-Hur* (1925) and *Don Juan* (1926). To play the love interest Hughes picked the appealing French actress Renée Adorée, whose charms had worked wonders in *The Big Parade*. In *The Mating Call* she appears as a Russian immigrant impounded on Ellis Island because she has no sponsor. A Florida farmer (Meighan) picks her for a bride simply because he wants a faithful, capable wife to replace the one (Evelyn Brent) who dumped him while he was away at war and who married a wealthier man (Alan Roscoe) in his absence. The man of wealth turns out not only to be a philandering cad, causing his wife to try and get back with her previous husband, but is the head of the local branch of the Ku Klux Klan. When a girl drowns in a pond on the farmer's property, the Klan tries him for murder, but it turns out that the head Klansman himself is the guilty party. Happily for the farmer, he also finds that he loves the adoring bride he chose on Ellis Island.

By 1928 standards of taste and interest the juicy story lines of *The Mating Call* added up to jingling coin at the box office. It was considered to be pretty hot stuff, with its scenes of sexual passion and frustration. Evelyn Brent was sultry as the woman willing to do anything to get back her ex-husband, and Renée Adorée pulsated in a demure sort of way as the grateful immigrant bride. Adorée had mastered the art of silent film acting, with intelligence as well as beauty. She was, however, a victim of film history. With her thick French accent and limited English, she could not make the transition from the silent era to the sound film. She was also a victim of her own vanity; in order to control her weight, she forced upon herself a ruinous diet that caused an eventual collapse. She died in 1933 at the age of thirty-five.

In a sense, Howard Hughes was also a victim of the film transition to sound. He had had, as he was sure he would have, two successful pictures in 1928 with *The Racket* and *The Mating Call*, and if all had gone as planned he would have been able to follow them the following year with the film on which he had spent so much time and money—*Hell's Angels*. All did not go as planned.

3

Hell's Angels

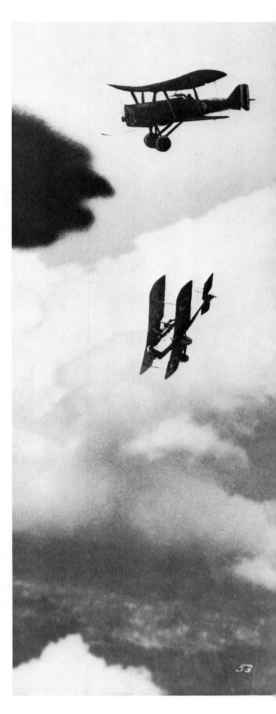

It was a long time after the armistice that Hollywood thought of making any pictures about the First World War. It had been such a horrible war, so brutal, sickening and disillusioning that the moviemakers rightly guessed the public would rather not be reminded of it. The sentiment began to change in 1924 when Maxwell Anderson and Laurence Stallings were successful on Broadway with their *What Price Glory?*, which took a realistic view of the misery of war and not the glory. It was also successful when made into a film, which led the film studios to reason that the war might be further exploited, albeit carefully. *The Big Parade* in 1925 proved the point.

Howard Hughes would undoubtedly have liked to have been the first man to make a movie about the aviators of that war. He certainly was not alone in his fascination with the subject. It was the only aspect of the war that had left intact any notion of military romanticism; most of it no longer a game for gentlemen—except in the air. There, at least in the beginning, knighthood had its last fling.

The first film to deal with First World War aviation was *Wings*, shot in 1926 and released the following year. It came about when writer John Monk Saunders, who had served as a pilot, took a story to Paramount's Jesse L. Lasky, who liked it. He retained Saunders as an advisor and hired William Wellman to direct. Wellman, then thirty, was the only Hollywood director to have seen active service as a pilot, having joined the Lafayette Flying Corps in 1916 and later transferred to the U.S. Army Air Service. His contributions helped make the expensive and lavishly produced *Wings* a major treatment of the subject matter. Such a success

Howard Hughes greets Captain Roscoe Turner on his arrival, along with his Sikorsky airplane, to join the *Hell's Angels* company. To the right of Turner are Greta Nissen and John Darrow. To the left of Hughes are Lucien Prival, Wallace Beery (purely a visitor) and Mrs. Turner.

might have deterred most anyone from making another such picture, especially right on its heels. Anyone, of course, other than Howard Hughes.

It was Marshall Neilan who both thought of the story concept and the title for *Hell's Angels*, knowing full well that it was exactly what the aviation-obsessed Hughes would readily accept. Hughes set up his production right away and contracted Neilan as director, which is precisely what Neilan had expected. He did not, however, expect the conditions under which he found himself working. When they had made *Everybody's Acting* together, Hughes had hovered in the background and kept his mouth shut. Now he hovered in the foreground and questioned Neilan, the actors and the cameramen on every decision.

Neilan quit after a few weeks and told Hughes to get himself another director. Hughes picked one with a reputation not only as a director but as an aviation authority, Luther Reed, who had been a writer on the subject for the *New York Herald-Tribune*. He appeared to be the best possible choice for such a film, but he, too, found Hughes constantly discussing every move. After two months, Reed threw in the towel, advising Hughes that since he seemed to know exactly what he wanted, he should direct it himself. Hughes decided to do just that.

Hughes hired scriptwriter Harry Behn to develop Neilan's slim outline into a screenplay. Behn had worked for him on *The Racket* and had recently made a good impression with his writing for *The Big Parade*. Hughes decided to shoot all the interiors and non-aerial sequences first, setting up production at the General Service Studios in Hollywood in October of 1927. These scenes were finished by the early

36

Hughes confers with his chief cameraman Harry Perry on dogfight maneuvers.

The young director takes a break.

The Howard Hughes Air Force and thirty-nine of his pilots, probably the largest private air force ever assembled, and all of it to re-fight the First World War.

Hell's Angels—the silent version, with Ben Lyon, Greta Nissen and James Hall.

part of the following January, although they had taken much longer than normal because of Hughes's laborious direction and his constant changes in the script and photography. The sequence of a ball in London took one week to shoot, with multiple takes. Hollywood legend has it that one piece of action was shot one hundred times. Even if partly true, it suggests an exhausting strain on the cast and crew.

The real substance of *Hell's Angels*, the aerial sequences, were begun within days of the studio episodes. The twenty-three-year-old Hughes may have exhausted his employees, but he himself showed so signs of wear. He could work for twenty and thirty hours at a stretch, and he seemed to show little regard for the more regular time schedules of other people. He never wore a watch and he appeared to be oblivious of time. In later years he would drive his executives to distraction by calling them at any hour during the night and expecting immediate conferences, but it was a cavalier habit that had manifested itself even in his early days as a movie producer. Hughes had an insatiable appetite for films and he would frequently call projectionists during the night and ask to see movies.

As a newly licensed pilot, Hughes probably imagined himself participating in the flying for *Hell's Angels*, but it was an idea quickly put aside. He hired veteran stunt pilot Frank Clarke to take command of the men who would fly the actual World War I planes which Hughes's buyers had brought in from all over Europe and America. In doing this, Hughes put together the largest private air force ever assembled. In time, legend would put the number of planes as high as eighty-seven, but the actual figure appears to be forty-five. These included a half-dozen

Hell's Angels—the sound version, with Jean Harlow replacing Greta Nissen. Ben Lyon remained.

Fokker D.VIIs, three S.E. 5s and five Thomas Morse S4C Scouts, which were modified to resemble the famous Sopwith Camels of the Royal Flying Corps. Hughes placed Harry Reynolds in charge of a ground crew of about thirty mechanics to restore, repair and service these planes.

The first base of operations was Mines Field in Inglewood, now the site of Los Angeles International Airport. Hughes used this field as the location for the British flying school sequences in the film, but he leased a tract of land at Van Nuys in the San Fernando Valley as the basis for his operation. This quickly became known as Caddo Field. However, it was at Mines Field in the first few days of aerial production that Hughes decided to try one of the Thomas Morse Scouts. Frank Clarke warned him not to, advising that the Morse had a rotary engine and that if the plane were sharply banked in the same direction as the rotation while near the ground it would spin dangerously. Hughes had asked Clarke, for dramatic effect, to do a banked take-off in the Morse and Clarke refused. Hughes then climbed into the plane, did a banked take-off, reached four hundred feet, spun and crashed. Said Clarke, "I thought for the moment that we had all lost our meal ticket."

Hughes was pulled from the plane in a dazed and bruised condition, and he spent a week in the hospital. It would be the first of several plane crashes over the years from which he would survive. One of the men who pulled Hughes from the wrecked Morse was a young Englishman who was then beginning his career in the movie business, Reggie Callow. *Hell's Angels* was his first job, as a general assistant, and over the next forty years Callow would become one of Hollywood's most respected assistant directors. Callow was interviewed in 1976 for the

41

American Film Institute by film historian Rudy Behlmer and he recalled being amazed by Hughes's first words when being pulled from the crash. "He was a bit out of his head and he said, 'That's another par hole I made. I shot a four on that one.' He was talking in golf language, because he was a superb golfer."

In making *Wings*, Paramount had sought and received government cooperation, resulting in the use of U.S. Army planes, flyers and airfields. Hughes, who could always be counted on to be contrary, decided that this was not the tack that he would follow. Reggie Callow, in the Behlmer interview, says, "He felt he could get better stuff without Army pilots, and that they weren't capable of doing the stunts that Hollywood stunt flyers could do. In those days several of the stunt flyers went around to county fairs doing those crazy stunts, such as wing-walking. Howard, I really thought, felt down in his heart that the stuff he wanted—planes spinning down out of control, spectacular dives, loops, crashes—would be done much better by these wild, crazy stunt pilots." Callow also recalled that Frank Clarke, fearful of the lives of his flyers, one day stormed up to Hughes and said, "Howard, I'm getting damn sick and tired of flying these planes—they're just held together with baling wire. One of these days one of us is going to get killed." Hughes responded, "Well, Frank, there's nothing wrong with the planes. It's you flyers." Says Callow, "All of a sudden there was a thump and we turned around. A motor had dropped out of one of the planes. It actually happened while we were sitting in the hangar—the motor fell out."

The risks taken by the stunt pilots in the making of *Hell's Angels* resulted in several crashes, particularly in forced landings, and the size of the Hughes air force became reduced. In the film's main aerial battle, only thirty planes were involved. Pilot Al Wilson had to bail out of his Fokker D.VII when his propeller suddenly dropped away from the engine. Wilson was flying in heavy fog at the time and assumed he was near the coast. He was actually directly over Hollywood. The propeller fell into Hollywood Boulevard, where fortunately it hit no one, and the plane fell, somewhat ironically, only two blocks from Grauman's Chinese Theatre, where the film would have its premiere. Wilson landed safely but painfully on the roof of a house.

Three men died during the making of *Hell's Angels*. The first was Al Johnson, when the plane he was flying hit high-tension wires as he was leaving Glendale Airport. He was instantly burned to death. C. K. Philips died when he ran out of gas while trying to reach a distant location; he was flying one of the S.E. 5s and tried to bring it down in a field on a deadstick (motorless) landing. The most horrifying death during the course of production was partly captured on film. It involved a large Sikorsky S-29A, which was doubling, with modifications, for a German Gotha bomber, since no Gothas were still intact by 1927.

The Sikorsky belonged to the flamboyant aviator Captain Roscoe Turner, who toured America and appeared at country fairs with his impressive airplane. Hughes hired both the plane and the owner, but Turner refused to perform the stunt in which the Gotha is shot down and

Hell's Angels: The ball sequence, with Ben Lyon, Jean Harlow, James Hall and Evelyn Hall.

spins to earth. It was extremely hazardous in such a large and unwieldy plane. Hughes called upon Hollywood's foremost crash pilot Dick Grace. He had hoped to employ Grace, who had been used all throughout the making of *Wings*, but Grace was not available during most of the time *Hell's Angels* was in production. Grace shook his head at the $250 offered by Hughes. He was, however, prepared to strike a bargain. If he could perform the stunt exactly as Hughes wished, then he would receive ten thousand dollars. Hughes shook his head at this and assigned the stunt to Al Wilson, who agreed to do it for one thousand dollars.

The Gotha incident was filmed on March 22, 1929, almost at the end of aerial production. In the plane with Wilson was mechanic Phil Jones, whose job it was to climb into the rear fusilage and release clouds of black smoke from pots containing a mixture of flour and lampblack when the Gotha was supposed to be hit. When Wilson put the Sikorsky into a simulated death plunge, he found it to be exactly that—the contortions caused the huge (it could carry fourteen passengers) plane to vibrate and Wilson lost control. He called for Jones to bail out and then jumped. Jones either did not hear the call or was unable to climb from the fuselage in time. He was in the plane when it dove into an orange grove from seven thousand feet.

The plunge of the Sikorsky-Gotha had been filmed but not the crash. To achieve this a Curtiss Jenny was altered to resemble a Gotha and pushed off a cliff. This incident was filmed near Oakland, as was the entire climactic air battle. Hughes found his main problem filming in southern California to be the lack of clouds. This did not occur to him until he had spent months and a great deal of money filming at the half

43

Hell's Angels: Douglas Gilmore, Jean
Harlow, James Hall and Ben Lyon.

dozen points he had set up in the San Fernando Valley, where in 1928 the skies were even cleaner and clearer than they are today—long before Los Angeles County became blighted by smog. It gradually occurred to Hughes that no matter how brilliant the photography and the flying, the action lacked a sense of speed and aerial perspective unless the planes moved by or through clouds. He spent a lot of time in the air looking for clouds in the vicinity, while his pilots and crew whiled away their time at Caddo Field, where the sign WAR POSTPONED—NO CLOUDS was posted for long periods of time.

The constant searching for clouds and the fragmentary results caused Hughes to transport his entire company to Oakland Airport in October of 1928. The area around San Francisco Bay was much more reliable "cloudwise." The move involved some one hundred men and massive equipment, plus forty airplanes. Hughes wanted only cumulous, billowing cloud formations, and this required a lot more waiting. The company worked at Oakland for four months, surely one of the longest and most costly location operations in film history. Throughout the long shooting schedule of *Hell's Angels*, calculated at about five thousand dollars per day, Hughes was constantly badgered by financier adviser Noah Dietrich and the top executives of Hughes Tool Company for what they considered a flagrant waste of funds. By this time the tool company had greatly expanded, manufacturing all kinds of mining equipment, and the profits were considerable. But the protestations fell on stubborn, deaf ears; "It's my money and I'll do what I like with it."

Hughes never allowed anyone but his staff to see any footage while the film was being made. Gossip columnist Louella Parsons sneaked into a screening room on one occasion and defied Hughes to throw her out. Years later, in an article she aptly titled *"The Man Nobody 'No's',"* she wrote, "I remember watching this picture being made. Even I was appalled at the way Howard was spending money. At one time he had twenty-four cameramen shooting battle scenes. Howard was creating his own war and it was almost as expensive as the real one."

The director of photography for *Hell's Angels* was Harry F. Perry, who had also served in that capacity for William Wellman on *Wings*. By this time in his life Perry had been a cinematographer for ten years and he was by far the top man in aviation photography. He brought in another ace aerial photographer, Elmer Dyer, as his chief assistant, with Tony Gaudio in charge of ground photography. With Frank Clarke, and a lot of imput from Hughes, Perry helped map out the aerial battles. The climactic battle between fifteen British and fifteen German fighter planes involved three weeks of intensive rehearsal for the pilots and photographers. That battle cost Hughes $300,000.

In an article by Oscar G. Estes in *Films in Review* (March, 1960), Perry recalled, "There were a lot of funny happenings before this big scene was completed, especially while we were working with the old stunt flyers. They would stay up most of the night, and then have to roll out at daylight to fly, for the early morning hours were best, since the rising sun was slow to burn off the morning clouds, which made the best

The German segment of the Hughes Air Force takes off from the west end of the San Fernando Valley, an area now entirely covered by housing.

backgrounds. One day Frank Clarke hired two flyers who were supposed to be unusually sharp and they went up to practice for the great dogfight scene. In about half an hour they were back on the ground. They said they wouldn't get mixed up with a crazy bunch of flyers like that for all the pay in the world."

Perry claimed that some of the most difficult shooting was that which involved Roscoe Turner's Sikorsky, which Turner piloted on every occasion but the fatal drive. Perry mounted several motor-driven, remote cameras in various parts of the aircraft in order to get shots of the two heroes, played by Ben Lyon and James Hall, as they flew the bomber with the idea of using it to bomb an ammunition dump. Turner piloted the plane from a set of controls out of camera range, and Perry flew on this, and all the other missions, to see that his aerial choreography was properly staged. Some of the dives of the mock Gotha had to be photographed from the ground.

"One shot I remember very well," said Perry, "was a dive down upon two motor-driven Mitchell cameras worth $5000 each. Turner had made half-a-dozen dives but none was close enough to the ground to suit Howard. So, on a Sunday morning, Roscoe told me he was really going to shave the cameras. He got the Gotha up in the air and started a steep dive from two thousand feet right at the cameras. He came too low and hit both of them, knocked them to pieces, broke both his props, and ended up in a beanfield a hundred yards beyond. The film was scattered all over the ground."

What amazed Perry was Hughes's reaction to all this. "He was playing golf that morning and had told me to call him when we obtained the shot. I phoned and got him on the ninth hole of the Lakeside course.

When I told him what had happened and that it would take a month to fix the Gotha, he laughed his head off and told me he would be out as soon as he had finished the eighteenth hole."

Harry Perry worked on *Hell's Angels* from October of 1927 until May of 1929, when it was thought the picture was completely finished. In one sense it was, and in another it was not. Perry was called back for six weeks' work in October and November, the reason being that Hughes had decided to remake large portions of his film. During the long course of production, sound had raised its voice on film. Al Jolson in *The Jazz Singer* had bellowed, "Wait a minute, folks, wait a minute—you ain't heard nothin' yet," and things would never be the same. Hughes knew this when he looked at his completed *Hell's Angels* and saw his lovely leading lady Greta Nissen mouthing soundless lines and his airplanes zipping around the skies noiselessly; he knew he had to re-make all the dramatic scenes and dub sound into the action sequences. So far *Hell's Angels* had cost him two million dollars, and to his business associates the only thing more horrifying than that was the realization that a lot more money would follow in its wake.

Replacing Greta Nissen was the first problem. The gorgeous Norwegian spoke with a thick accent, and since she was supposed to be playing an English girl it was impossible to use her in the new version. Hughes characteristically took his time about picking a replacement. He considered an established actress, Ann Harding, but dismissed her as too genteel, and he tested a fledgling named Carole Lombard, but thought her not sexy enough. There were hundreds of others. It was his leading man, Ben Lyon, who brought him Jean Harlow. She was then eighteen and in the year she had been in Hollywood, having arrived from her native Kansas City, she had played bits in Charlie Chaplin's *City Lights*, Laurel and Hardy's *Double Whoopee*, and had received eleventh billing in a Paramount comedy, *The Saturday Night Kid*, which starred Clara Bow and one of the stars of *Hell's Angels*, James Hall. Hall had had plenty of time to do this picture during the long haul of the Hughes's film, whereas Ben Lyon, who had been borrowed from First National, did nothing else—except perhaps wonder what this long gap would do for his popularity.

Lyon spotted Harlow on a sound stage as she was doing a dance sequence. He asked her to come with him as soon as she finished the scene, which she did, complete with the black satin gown worn for the scene. At first sight Hughes was not impressed. He said to Lyon, "Are you kidding?" Lyon insisted that this was the girl. Hughes then told him to go ahead and make a test with her, to direct it and do it before the day was out. The results got Harlow the part and a salary of $125 a week.

To write a new script for the sound portions, Hughes hired Joseph Moncure March, and to direct them he chose James Whale, who had just arrived in Hollywood after directing with great success in both London and New York the First World War drama *Journey's End*. Directing the film version of that fine play started Whale's distinguished career as a movie director. His and March's first reaction on viewing Hughes's

47

picture was one of depression. They both thought that aside from the splendid aerial sequences and the ending, the material was feeble. Whale and March talked Hughes into letting them take a new approach with the material. Hughes, by now truly concerned about his mammoth undertaking, readily agreed. The decision was also taken to shoot portions of the film in color, principally the ball sequence. One of Hughes's new business interests was a company titled Multi-Color, but it was one he was advised to drop because the making of color film was at that time too expensive. Nonetheless, the color portions of *Hell's Angels* served a good purpose.

So did Jean Harlow, although at the outset both Whale and March agonized over her lack of dramatic ability. She had had no training as an actress and being given such a role in a film of this scope must have been extremely hard for her. She was, however, a willing pupil and a hard worker. Despite her deficiencies on the dramatic level, the Hughes film made her an instant star. With her platinum hair, sensuous figure and cheeky sexuality, she clicked with the public immediately, especially when she spoke the line that would become one of Hollywood's glorious clichés: "Would you be shocked if I put on something more comfortable?" Since she said this to Ben Lyon while wearing a flimsy, revealing evening gown, it was a line that could hardly miss its mark.

Since Hughes had by this time already acquired a reputation as a young man with a taste for lovely young girls, it was assumed in Hollywood, ever ready to believe anything lascivious, that the producer was having an affair with his leading lady. They were seen together in public but Harlow much later confessed to a journalist that there was never any personal relationship. She said, "He's got a lot of charm in his own funny way. But he never mixes business with pleasure. As far as I'm concerned, I might be another airplane. He expects you to work the same way—never get tired, give your best performance at any hour of the day or night, and never think about anything else. The nearest he ever came to making a pass at me was offering me a bite of a cookie." Hughes never again used her in a film, but for two years he loaned her to other studios, clearly at a profit, until he decided to end his own career as a film producer in 1932, when he sold her contract to MGM.

When finally completed in early 1930, *Hell's Angels* ran one minute short of two hours. When it was re-released a generation later it was trimmed to ninety minutes, which is the version most likely seen when viewed today. None of the aerial sequences were cut from the re-release, which would have been foolish since the concensus, arrived at almost from the day it first appeared, was that the aviation footage was what gave the film its rightful place in film history and that the plotlines, the dialogue, and the acting were of a kind that would have made *Hell's Angels* a mere programmer minus the aerial wizardry.

The script had gone through convolutions in the two and a half years of production and it must have been difficult for Hughes, Neilan, Behn, Estabrook and March to recognize who had done what and how. What the public saw was the story of two brothers, Monte (Lyon) and

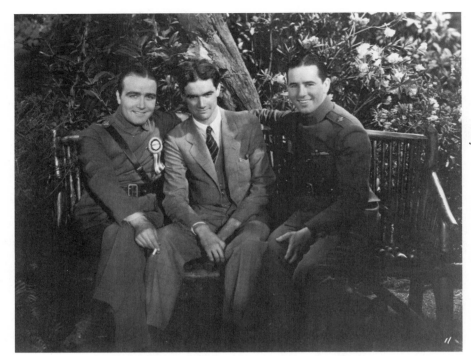

Howard Hughes with his two stars, James Hall and Ben Lyon.

Roy Rutledge (Hall), who are students at Oxford University when the war breaks out in 1914. Among their friends is an idealistic young German, Karl Arnstedt (John Darrow), who reluctantly returns to the Fatherland to serve the Kaiser, because he loves the English and their country. The brothers are different in character; Roy is solid, sensible and dependable, and Monte is not. There is a softness in his spine. Just prior to the war Monte had had an affair with the wife of a German aristocrat, Baron von Kranz (Lucien Prival), and when challenged to a duel he denied knowing the woman.

With British lads flocking to the colors, Roy joins the Royal Flying Corps, with Monte somewhat sheepishly following in his footsteps a little while later. At a charity ball in London Monte becomes infatuated with Roy's fiancée Helen (Harlow), a flighty society girl who does not really love Roy but feels she must pretend to do so in the national interest. This does not stop her from inviting the handsome Monte to her apartment, where she beguilingly slips into something "more comfortable." Months later, when she goes to France to serve as a canteen girl and makes eyes at a variety of young officers, it gradually dawns upon Roy that his fiancée is really a floozy, despite her social breeding, and not worth marrying. The decision is not one that bothers Helen.

The scene following Monte's seduction discreetly fades to black and dissolves into one of the truly great episodes of *Hell's Angels*, the bombing attack of the Zeppelin on London. The huge, sinister airship silently glides through the clouds at night and comes to a halt over the British capital. The seemingly maniacal commander lowers his observer's small compartment (somewhat resembling a motorcycle sidecar) from a steel

49

The mighty Zeppelin of *Hell's Angels*, actually a sixty-foot-long model.

cable. The observer is none other than Karl Arnstedt, who hates his assignment. When he is lowered several hundred feet below the clouds he realizes that he is entirely responsible for the placement of the bombs. By telephone he gives the signal to drop the bombs, which all land harmlessly in a body of water. The commander, delighted in the belief he has obliterated Trafalgar Square, orders the Zeppelin to return home. His expression quickly changes when he learns he is being attacked by four British fighters, two of which are piloted by the Rutledge brothers. The commander, desperate to lighten his load, cuts the cable from which Karl is suspended, sending him to his death. He then orders all manner of equipment jettisoned. Next he orders half his crew to jump into the dark abyss below. One by one the German airmen, *"Für Kaiser und Vaterlund,"* do as ordered. Three of the British fighters are damaged and break off, including the Rutledge brothers, but the fourth sacrifices his life by crashing into the Zeppelin and causing it to burst into flames.

The Zeppelin episode of *Hell's Angels* remains one of the most spectacular and convincing pieces of aerial warfare ever filmed. It was based on an actual occurrence, when a Zeppelin was brought down by an RFC lieutenant named Warneford, who received a posthumous Victoria Cross. There is, however, no record of any German airmen being ordered to jump to their deaths, but in the Hollywood of the late Twenties, Germans were still being depicted as the Beastly Huns, a characterization from which profit is still drawn.

The Zeppelin episode was directed by E. Roy Davidson, a master of photographic effects, who constructed two sixty-foot-long models and filmed them in a vast balloon hangar in Arcadia, on a U.S. Army airfield that is now the site of the Santa Anita Racetrack. Among Davidson's crew was an engineer who had worked for the Zeppelin company during the war, and he supervised the construction of the models. Artificial clouds were created in the hangar and the models were suspended from an overhead trolley-like rig. At one end of the hangar Davidson built full-scale sections of Zeppelin interiors, including a complete control room. A half-dozen cameras filmed from all angles, and when the Zeppelin exploded in flames, one shot, taken from beneath a glass floor, gave the impression that the blazing wreck was falling on the audience. It is a sequence that has never been equalled, and it is surprising how much this footage resembles the newsreel shots of the destruction of the Hindenburg several years later. The sequence, shot silent, cost Hughes $460,000 and it took no persuasion to convince him that it should not be done again. German-speaking actors were brought in to dub the voices.

Following some forgettable scenes of romance and humor in the French canteens and barracks, *Hell's Angels* moves into its real glory, the concluding battle between the Allied and German fighter pilots and the destruction by the heroes of the vast German munitions depot. A British general addresses the assembled pilots and explains that the Allied ground push cannot be undertaken unless the depot is destroyed. The Rutledge brothers volunteer to fly a captured Gotha, complete with its German markings, which makes it relatively simple to reach the target

James Hall and Ben Lyon with Captain Roscoe Turner in front of his Sikorsky, made up to look like a Gotha bomber. Note the camera rig mounted over the right engine. This proud and mighty airplane was just about to make its final flight.

and destroy it. Making the return is another matter, since the bombing has been observed by a squadron commanded by none other than the celebrated Baron Manfred von Richthofen. The Allied planes engage in a fierce battle with the Germans, but it does not prevent the offending Gotha from being shot down.

When captured, the brothers are intensely questioned about the expected Allied thrust. Monte finds himself faced by an old adversary, Baron von Kranz, and to save his life the weak Monte agrees to tell what he knows. Roy also agrees, but it is a ruse; in exchange for the information, Roy asks for a revolver with a single bullet, with which he will be able to erase his dishonor. Instead he shoots his brother, who, when dying in Roy's arms speaks his last words, "Don't cry, it was the only thing you could do." Moments later, as Roy is marched off for summary execution, he cries, "I'll be with you in just a moment, Monte." As the shots of the firing squad fade away, the scene moves to the shattered landscape of the western front, with its endless trenches, barbed wire and lines of soldiers at the ready. With cheers they swarm into the offensive.

The dogfight between the fighter pilots, involving thirty planes, not only was the most astonishing aerial warfare filmed to that time, but nothing done since has surpassed it. If Howard Hughes had been responsible for nothing in film annals other than this, he would still deserve an honorable mention. His pilots and photographers achieved a breathtaking sequence, with the planes ferociously attacking each other like angry hornets, zipping, swooping, looping and tumbling. It is amazing that none of the pilots were killed in filming this material. The

51

The final scene of *Hell's Angels*, the Allied push, for which Hughes hired 1700 uniformed extras and then edited the sequence to barely twenty seconds.

on-screen, head-on collision between two of the fighters was done with models with twelve-foot wingspans. This was the work of E. Roy Davidson, who also planned and directed the elaborate and brilliant destruction of the ammunition depot.

Hell's Angels received its premiere at Grauman's Chinese Theatre in Hollywood on the evening of May 27, 1930. Hughes was intent upon the most glittering and impressive premiere possible, and to this end he had the wholehearted cooperation of master showman Sid Grauman. A goodly portion of Hollywood Boulevard was blocked off and the thousands of spectators gawked as almost every celebrity in Hollywood drove up in their limousines. They especially gawked at the sight of slinky Jean Harlow in a gown that appeared to have been sewn on her. Hundreds of searchlights swept the skies, as planes buzzed the boulevard and several men descended by parachute. The film received a standing ovation, topping off an evening that justified, at least in the mind of Howard Hughes, the vast amount of time and money spent.

The cost of the film—salaries, film stock, developing, and production costs, including a half million dollars spent on purchasing and maintaining planes—came to almost four million dollars. This did not include prints, publicity, and promotion. The cost would be difficult to compute in terms of today's costs, but it might well be ten times more. The only film which had even approached the Hughes film in cost had been MGM's mammoth production of *Ben-Hur*, released in 1925. *Hell's Angels* was an immediate success, with long bookings at major theatres, and it did particularly well in England, where some of the critics described it as a masterpiece, despite the fact that its three obviously American stars were trying to be British. Had it not been for the fantastic

Graumann's Chinese Theatre and
Hollywood Boulevard on the evening of
May 27, 1930—the premiere of *Hell's
Angels*, the like of which would never be
seen again.

aerial sequences, the London critics might have been less charitable about the accents of Harlow, Lyon and Hall.

Apart from its merits and demerits, *Hell's Angels* holds a record never broken. During its long production, its photographers shot miles of film. The average ninety-minute movie runs to approximately eight thousand feet of film, and the average director films his material at a ratio of about ten-to-one. Some of the most painstaking and demanding of Hollywood's famous directors, men like George Stevens and George Cukor, and England's David Lean, have sometimes shot twenty times as much footage as they needed. For *Hell's Angels* Hughes ended up with three hundred times as much footage as he needed. How hard his editors worked can only be imagined, especially with the finicky Hughes leaning over their shoulders.

Hughes always maintained that *Hell's Angels* was a hugely profitable picture. Noah Dietrich, some years after his bitter parting with Hughes, claimed it barely covered its enormous costs. It was released at a particularly bad time, just months after the stock market crash that plunged America into its great depression, although it was a depression that blighted almost every industry but motion pictures. For all that, Dietrich and the men who managed Hughes Tool Company breathed a gigantic sigh of relief when *Hell's Angels* finally stopped draining their funds. The tool company, by 1929 an immensely successful operation, was seriously affected by the slump in the oil industry, but it was never in danger of being wiped out. On the other hand, it might have been had Hughes come up with another *Hell's Angels*.

Hughes, a mere twenty-five when the film was finished but a much less naïve and far tougher man than he had been before he started it, never held back on giving credit to the men who had worked for him in making *Hell's Angels*. Despite having achieved exactly what he said he would do—become a big name in the picture business—he did not, to Hollywood's puzzlement, act like a big name. He was still shy, socially awkward and quiet. But he shocked Hollywood with his modesty and honesty in a 1932 interview when he confessed, "Making *Hell's Angels* by myself was my biggest mistake. It would have been finished sooner and cost less. I had to worry about money, sign checks, hire pilots, get planes, cast everything, direct the whole thing. Trying to do the work of twelve men was just dumbness on my part. I learned by bitter experience that no one man can know everything."

To his business associates and all those who would be called upon to work with Hughes on future movies, it sounded as if the amazing young man had learned some lessons. Perhaps in the future he would delegate authority and allow underlings to do their jobs without interference. Perhaps.

Love and Celluloid

With best wishes,
Billie Dove

Not long after Ella Rice Hughes decided to return to Houston and terminate her impossible marriage, her husband met Billie Dove, who would be the first of an incredibly long line of beautiful movie stars with whom Howard Hughes would fall in love. The departing wife had no way of knowing it, but the treatment she received from Hughes was a pattern he would follow with all the ladies. It always began with instant interest, almost obsessive, with lots of romantic attention, and then diminuendo leading to a cool ending.

When Hughes first arrived in Hollywood he was still a gangling youth. By the time he had made *Hell's Angels* and had become a Hollywood celebrity, lauded by a community whose idol has always been success, the gangling quality had matured to the point of being rather appealing. He had put a little more weight on his six-foot-three frame, and a filling out of his facial features had produced a handsome face, complete with dark eyes and hair. He was at that point tall, dark and handsome, and the fact that he was also famous, shy and diffident of manner made him attractive to women.

Billie Dove was four years older than Hughes. She first set eyes on him at a party and was not impressed by his casual manner of dress, which, it is said, included tennis shoes. Hughes senior had been an elegant, fashion-plate kind of man, but Hughes junior, perhaps because he felt he could not live up to the father he so admired, went in the

Cock of the Air, with Billie Dove and Chester Morris.

opposite sartorial direction. As time went by he seemed to care less and less about appearances. But if Dove was not impressed at that first meeting, she soon became impressed with his immediate courtship.

By the time of that meeting in early 1929 she had been in movies for eight years. With her exceptional teenage beauty she had been a top artists' model, posing for magazine covers and advertisements. Florenz Ziegfeld offered her a part in his *Follies of 1917*, which began an instantly successful career. Four years later, age twenty, she went to Hollywood and at the time of meeting Hughes she had starred in forty films. She was then the wife of director Irvin Willat, but the marriage had long been on-again, off-again and by September of 1929 she had announced a final separation. Hughes started his romantic campaign with jewels and bushels of flowers, and made it difficult for any other man to court her.

Among Dove's boyfriends was George Raft, then at the start of his movie career. One evening when they were together in a suite at the Ambassador Hotel, Raft received a phone call from a friend in the lobby, advising him that Hughes was also there and that he was asking for the number of the suite. No novice actor is likely to run in opposition to a film producer, especially one who is a millionaire, and Raft slipped out of the hotel by a side door. This proved to be a provident move, because it was Hughes's choice of Raft for *Scarface* that lifted Raft into stardom.

Another boyfriend became intimidated when he took Dove on a picnic and found the site being buzzed by Hughes in his little airplane. Hughes then landed nearby and invited himself to join the couple. It was hard for either Dove or the boyfriend not to be impressed, although for different reasons. Hughes had found out where they were picnicking because he had had them trailed. Billie Dove thus became the first movie actress to be subjected to a process that would become standard practice with all Hughes's Hollywood loves—surveillance. He employed operatives and private detectives to keep tabs on his women; he wanted to know where they were and if anyone else might be interested in them, and he also had them investigated for their medical records. He was vitally concerned about the health of those with whom he was in close contact.

Hollywood had reason to believe that Hughes's courtship of Dove would lead to marriage, especially when the rumor got around that he had given Irvin Willat a quarter of a million dollars to get a divorce as soon as possible. Willat denied this at the time, but toward the end of his life he admitted that it was even more than a quarter million. Noah Dietrich claimed that the sum was $325,000 and that it was paid in one-thousand-dollar bills. After this transaction Hughes flew Dove to Nevada so that she could establish the six weeks of residence necessary for a divorce. He then encouraged her to terminate her contract with First National Pictures, which she did. Hughes signed Billie Dove to a contract with Caddo Productions, with the intention of turning a popular movie star into a superstar.

The Age for Love was the film with which Hughes hoped to elevate the career of the actress he adored. He carefully looked around for the right project and finally picked up the rights to the novel of that title by

Matt Moore and Chester Morris in *Cock of the Air.*

Ernest Pascal, and hired the novelist to adapt his work into a screenplay. To make sure the script would be really good, he then brought in playwright Robert E. Sherwood to supply the dialogue. The well-regarded Frank Lloyd was hired as director. The fact that Hughes hired Sherwood was an indication of his cool business judgment, which assessed a man's ability rather than how he might have felt about him personally. It was Sherwood who had refused to be swayed by the euphoric consensus on *Hell's Angels* and said instead, "One shouldn't jump to a natural conclusion that it is an extra-ordinarily fine picture because it isn't. If the lamentable truth must be known, it is pretty much of a mess. It is one of the most exciting news stories that the cinema has ever evolved, and therein lies the secret of its terrific appeal." Any other movie producer would have shunned the bearer of such a lukewarm assessment. Not Hughes.

If the first review of *The Age for Love* read by Hughes was the one in the November 17, 1931, edition of *Variety*, he may have gulped over its opening paragraph: "Everybody makes mistakes and this is one by Howard Hughes. It takes 81 minutes to tell practically nothing, meanwhile giving no indication of chances for anything better through cutting. At the New York Rivoli it was razzed by the audience." In this tame drama of married life, Dove is a bride who decides she does not want a child, much to the chagrin of her husband (Charles Starrett). He loves her but asks for a divorce when she remains adamant about children, her views on family life having been gauged from the unhappy examples she has witnessed. The husband then marries a woman who is

57

The Age for Love, with Charles Starrett, Adrian Morris, Lois Wilson and Billie Dove.

eager to have a child, and does, but both realize they do not truly love each other. The second wife gallantly departs with her child, leaving the way open for the husband to rejoin the woman he does truly love, who by this time has come to her senses. The critical drubbing of the film was uniform, with some praise for the way the lovely Dove handled Sherwood's dialogue.

If Dove was hurt by the failure of *The Age for Love*, she kept her feelings to herself. She was not a talkative woman anyway. Many in Hollywood thought she and Hughes were a good match because he was slightly hard of hearing and she never had much to say. When a reporter asked about her feelings for Hughes, she replied, "I have nothing to say," but she did allow that he was a brilliant pilot and a first-class golfer, and that she greatly enjoyed her flying lessons. Hughes had arranged for J. B. Alexander, the man who had been his aeronautical adviser on *Hell's Angels*, to give her lessons, and she later received a pilot's license. In that regard she was probably closer to Hughes than any other woman he ever knew in Hollywood. For a period of at least one year they seemed to be inseparable.

For the second Billie Dove picture Hughes reasoned that something dealing with aviation might be viable, especially as she now knew how to fly. And in setting the film in the First World War he could at least save money by drawing on his huge *Hell's Angels* library of out-takes. He retained the services of Robert E. Sherwood, who, in company with Charles Lederer, turned out a romantic adventure titled *Cock of the Air.* Hughes liked it and hired Tom Buckingham to direct it, and cast the popular Chester Morris as a dashing young American aviator, Lt. Roger Craig, who falls victim to the allure of seductive French actress Lilli de Rousseau (Dove, of course).

Cock of the Air begins in Paris, where Lilli is idolized by hordes of Allied officers, so much so that the Allied High Command becomes fearful that they are neglecting their duties. For the good of the war effort, Lilli is asked by representatives of the Allied governments to leave Paris and go to Italy, where she may perhaps be less of a distraction. In Venice the situation is not much different from Paris; a group of admiring army officers welcomes her with a bouquet and attends her during a carnival. Among those in attendance is Roger Craig, who has a reputation as a ladies' man. Lilli finds this amusing and challenging, and accepts his invitation to dine with him in his rented villa. During their first evening Roger is a little too confidant and Lilli slaps him down. In a rage he retires to his bedroom, but a little while later he finds her serenading him under his window. She promises to wait for him as he gets dressed, but then vanishes into the night.

Lilli's playfulness is halted when she receives news that the understudy who took over her stage play in Paris has become greatly successful in it. Roger volunteers to fly her to Paris when she explains she has personal reasons for an immediate return, although he is still unaware that she is a famous actress. In flying Lilli to Paris, Roger ignores his military duties and an order is put out for his arrest. In Paris the lovers go through a series of tiffs and misunderstandings, mostly due to Lilli's not wanting to reveal her identity to him. He finally discovers that his mysterious beauty is a celebrated actress and that she has enough influence with the high ranking military to clear the charges against him and get him a special assignment, which happily coincides with her receiving even greater acclaim in her play.

Cock of the Air met with only mild response from the critics and the public. Those expecting more aviation footage in a picture with such a title were disappointed, since it had little besides the flight between Italy and Paris, and the pre-release rumors of some sexy moments between the battling lovers led to further disappointment when the censors ordered several minutes clipped from the picture. For Billie Dove it must have been a time of confusion. Her wealthy producer-lover had starred her in two films that had made little impact, and by the time *Cock of the Air* was completed she was seeing less and less of him. He was still tender and attentive, but only intermittently. He would, she later confessed, arrive and depart without announcement or explanation, with no regard for time, and that he often simply disappeared for days. In other words, she had been treated in the same manner as the wife from whom Hughes was now divorced and on whom he had made a settlement of over one million dollars. It was a pattern that would be repeated over and over.

Billie Dove's contract with Hughes called for five films, but once it was apparent that he was no longer interested in her either personally or professionally she agreed to a termination and a final payment of

IS THERE A SUBSTITUTE FOR LOVE?

Howard Hughes
PRESENTS
"The AGE FOR LOVE"
FROM ERNEST PASCAL'S SENSATIONAL NOVEL
WITH
BILLIE DOVE · CHARLES STARRE
LOIS WILSON · MARY DUNCA
EDWARD EVERETT HORTO
A
FRANK LLOYD PRODUCTIC

WATCH FOR NEWSPAPER ANNOUNCEMEN

• As interesting as "Hell's Angels" —as true to life as "The Front Page," this great picture answers the question—"Can the HOME survive modernism?"

• It is a modern picture based on the day's most common problem—should the young wife work? It will grip you— interest you— entertain you—let you see behind the scenes of life's greatest drama.

• "The Age For Love" is now ready for release. Take the whole family for a memorable evening's enjoyment.

"UNITED ARTISTS PICTURE"

Billie Dove and Charles Starrett in *The Age for Love.*

$100,000. After that she never ever saw him again. She made only one more film, *Blondie of the Follies,* co-starring with Marion Davies and Robert Montgomery, after which she decided to end her career. During the making of the film she met and fell in love with a handsome young millionaire named Robert Kenaston, part of whose fortune came from oil, and married him in May of 1933. They were married for thirty-seven years. Like most of the women with whom Hughes was romantically attached, she declines to talk about him. When he died she was approached for comment by many reporters, but she refused to speak to any of them.

Howard Hughes's interest in aviation had steadily grown since he took up residence in Hollywood. When not making films, playing golf or courting women, he was either flying or studying aircraft construction. He could often be found wearing overalls in some aircraft hangar or repair shop, standing over an engine he was taking apart, looking like an ordinary young working man. At times like this there was nothing about his bearing and manner to lead anyone to believe that this was a man with an instantly recognizable name, a man who produced movies in Hollywood.

He appeared little perturbed by the failure of *The Age for Love* and *Cock of the Air,* or the departure of Billie Dove from his life. Hughes did not then or ever reveal his personal feelings. He could always lose himself in business interests. At the start of 1931 he set about making *The Front Page,* but he also put into production another picture in which he could utilize some of his *Hell's Angels* footage. Its title, *Sky Devils,* led moviegoers to believe something epic awaited them. What they got was a lightweight service comedy, using some of the marvelous dogfight footage and portions of the destruction of the ammunition depot from *Hell's Angels.* Afterwards Hughes leased his *Hell's Angels* aviation footage, portions of which turned up in *The White Sister* (1933), *Today We Live* (1933), *Crimson Romance* (1934), *Hell in the Heavens* (1934), *Suzy* (1936) and *Army Surgeon* (1942). It is interesting to note that most of the two dozen or so black-and-white Hollywood movies dealing with First World War aviation and made between 1927 and 1942 used stock footage from either *Hell's Angels* or *Wings.* Hollywood did not touch the subject again until 1958 when William Wellman directed *Lafayette Escadrille,* which, like all such films made since then, was shot in color.

Numerous people had approached Hughes with ideas about movies dealing with the First World War. One of them was Edward Sutherland, a director who had been in Hollywood since 1914 and who had a flair for comedy. In company with Joseph Moncure March he had devised a story about a couple of soldiers who end up in the Army Air Service and create comedic havoc. Hughes liked the concept and hired a half-dozen writers to flesh it out with dialogue. To head the cast he borrowed Spencer Tracy from the Fox Studio. Tracy, who had distinguished himself as a stage actor in New York, had by this time made five movies, including *Goldie,* for which Hughes had leased Jean Harlow to Fox. *Sky Devils* gave the young Tracy his first crack at knockabout comedy, and if nothing else it

Sky Devils, with Ann Dvorak, Spencer
Tracy and Bill Boyd.

Sky Devils: Spencer Tracy, Yola D'Avril
and Bill Boyd.

61

Spencer Tracy and Ann Dvorak in *Sky Devils*.

persuaded him to avoid the form in the future. Hughes assigned George Cooper as his buddy, and he confused moviegoers somewhat by hiring William Boyd as the tough sergeant. But this was not the William Boyd who had done so well as one of the *Two Arabian Knights.* This was a stage actor of that name and in order to tell them apart Hollywood dubbed him William "Stage" Boyd. Sadly for him but fortunately for film historians, this Boyd died in 1935 at the age of forty-five, at the time the other one made the first of the Hopalong Cassidy pictures. "Stage" Boyd was the original Sergeant Quirt in the play *What Price Glory?* and it is as a rough Quirt-like character that he appears in *Sky Devils.* He later appeared as Bill Sikes in the filming of *Oliver Twist* (1933), but this, like all his films, usually appears in the film credits of William "Hopalong Cassidy" Boyd.

Spencer Tracy and Ann Dvorak in *Sky Devils.*

Sky Devils opens with Wilkie (Tracy) and Mitchell (Cooper) joining the army after losing their jobs as lifeguards when it is discovered neither knows how to swim. Their plan on joining is to desert, but in trying to do so they end up on a ship bound for France, where they are assigned as mechanics in the air service. Their constant conflict with their hard-hearted sergeant becomes more strained when Wilkie and the sergeant vie for the attentions of a pretty girl (Ann Dvorak). While roaming around without leave, Wilkie and Mitchell accidentally destroy a German ammunition depot, which causes them to be greeted as heroes when they return to camp. But in demonstrating how they achieved the destruction of the enemy depot, they in a similar manner cause havoc and heavy damage at their own air station.

Sky Devils was received by the moviegoers as just another slapstick service farce, replete with air crashes, car chases, barroom brawls and obvious humor. One critic suggested that it was a *What Price Glory?* of the air as seen through the eyes of a Mack Sennett. As program product it came and went, and caused Hollywood to wonder if the wonder boy really had any judgment about the making of movies. He soon cleared the air of doubts with a pair of pictures that would become part of film history.

On the set of *The Front Page*, with Pat
O'Brien, Mary Brian, and director Lewis
Milestone examining a pistol.

5

Newspapermen and Gangsters

Cock of the Air, The Age for Love and *Sky Devils* were all disappointing movies. They played their theatre bookings with little response and mild reviews, and to Hollywood it seemed as if Hughes was having trouble coming up with something that would raise his drooping flag as a film producer. As on prior occasions, and many thereafter, opinions about his probable failure were proven wrong. With *The Front Page* and *Scarface*, Hughes became responsible for two films, one about the newspaper business and the other about organized crime, that would not only win praise and profit but would have profound bearing upon the style of many other movies dealing with those subjects.

The Front Page was among the most successful Broadway plays of 1928. Its authors, Ben Hecht and Charles MacArthur, were paid $125,000 for the screen rights, but when Hughes asked them if that included adapting the play into a scenario, they replied in the negative and asked for an additional $80,000. Hughes thought this unreasonable, and since the pair would not settle for less, he assigned the scripting to Bartlett Cormack and Charles Lederer. Hecht had won an Oscar in 1927 for his screenplay *Underworld*, but in the opinion of Hughes that did not entitle him to a huge salary adapting one of his own plays. But Hecht and MacArthur made no objection to the respected Cormack and Lederer, who assured the original authors that their treatment would be an almost literal version of the play, with most of the changes being visual. To this end they were well served by Lewis Milestone.

The Front Page, with Pat O'Brien, Edward
Everett Horton and Walter Catlett.

Milestone had recently won a second Oscar, for his spectacular
directing of *All Quiet on the Western Front*, which among other things
was notable for quick, mobile camera movements. Under the terms of
his contract with Hughes he was committed to one more film; he
jumped at Hughes's offer to direct *The Front Page* because it was a
challenge. Instead of a vast battlefield on which to work, *The Front Page*
was limited for the most part to a single set. How, wondered Hollywood,
could he get movement out of that confinement? When viewed today it
must be remembered that the film was made in 1931, not long after the
start of the sound era, and that the primitive recording devices had
almost robbed movies of the mobility they had previously achieved. With
his direction of *The Front Page*, Milestone proved that mobility was
possible on a small set, and that if the actors were restricted in their
movements, then the camera should move. One of the most notable
things about this film is the use of the tracking camera, energetically
moving in time to the rapid dialogue and backed up with quick,
imaginative film editing. The pacing, like the subject material itself, is
almost ruthless.

Hecht and MacArthur had both been newspapermen and *The Front
Page* is clearly a play drawn from first-hand observation. It just as clearly
is a dramatic and comedic exaggeration of all they had ever seen and
heard in the harsh world of journalism. As viewed by Hecht-MacArthur
it is a world populated by cynical reporters, heartless editors and corrupt
politicians. Everyone is trying to outwit everybody else and in many
instances doing it with glee. *The Front Page*, running 101 minutes, is like
watching a journalistic equivalent of a football game.

The two leading characters are the scheming, calculating editor Walter Burns (Adolphe Menjou) and his top reporter, the glib, facile Hildy Johnson (Pat O'Brien). Theirs has long been a bantering, Flagg-and-Quirt relationship, but now Hildy has had enough of being overworked, taken advantage of, lied to, worked ridiculous hours and forced to take ridiculous risks. He intends to quit the paper and marry Peggy (Mary Brian), who does not want her intended involved in such a brutal business. Burns bears down hard on Hildy to tackle at least one last job, that of covering the hanging of a woebegone clerk named Earl Williams (George E. Stone), who for some reason he cannot explain took leave of his dim senses and shot a policeman.

George E. Stone and Pat O'Brien in *The Front Page.*

The setting is the dingy press room of the Criminal Courts Building in Chicago. A dozen or so bored reporters pass the time playing cards, telling jokes, inventing alibis for each other when their wives call, and grabbing the phone whenever they have anything to relate to their editors. There does not seem to be an ounce of compassion for humankind among the lot of them. Before leaving for New York with his bride, Hildy drops by to say goodbye to his flippant fellow newshawks. Someone else who drops by is Molly (Mae Clarke), the prostitute girlfriend of Williams. Before jumping from the window in a suicide attempt, she tells the reporters what a crude and heartless bunch she thinks they are. She also implies, with some merit, that their callous attitude is partly responsible for Williams's sentence. To them he is just another story.

Hearing that Williams has escaped, the reporters leave the room and follow the police, all except Hildy, who is not interested—until Williams accidentally stumbles into the press room and Hildy realizes that he has an exclusive. He also realizes from what Williams tells him that he has proof of the corruption in local government, involving the Mayor (James Gordon) and Sheriff Hartman (Clarence Wilson), both of whom are up for re-election and know their chances are nil unless Williams is immediately recaptured and hanged. Their guilt is increased by their having bribed a messenger (Slim Summervile), who carries a reprieve for Williams from the governor, to get lost. When Burns learns of the situation, he promises Hildy that if he sticks with the story he will afterwards cheerfully release him from his job and send the bridal pair on their way to New York with his blessings.

While the other reporters and the police are searching the city, Hildy promises to help Williams. When he hears the others coming back to the room, he hides the pitiful fugitive in the top of a large roll-top desk. Burns arrives and with Hildy he devises a scheme that will not only save Williams from the gallows but reveal the sheriff and the mayor as the venal characters they are. The scheme appears to go awry when Williams is discovered in the desk. Burns and Hildy are arrested and handcuffed as accessories, but the governor's messenger then reappears, having decided duty is more important than a bribe, and the situation is resolved. Burns, appearing to keep his promise to Hildy that he will release him, makes the bridegroom a gift of his gold watch. After Hildy

67

Clarence H. Wilson, James Gordon, Pat O'Brien and Adolphe Menjou, in *The Front Page.*

and Peggy leave to catch their train Burns calls the police in New York to arrest Hildy because, "The son of a bitch just stole my watch." The journalistic career of Hildy is likely to continue under the same shrewd boss.

Ben Hecht claimed that he patterned the role of Walter Burns on a Chicago editor he had known, Walter Howie. Said Hecht: "Howie had a glass eye, and it was easy to spot because it was the one with the warmth." On Broadway Burns had been played by Osgood Perkins (the father of Anthony Perkins) but he was not considered strong enough for the film version. The actor Hughes wanted for Burns, with instant agreement on the part of Lewis Milestone, was the rough, gruff Louis Wolheim. It was Milestone who was responsible for Pat O'Brien playing Hildy Johnson in the film, despite O'Brien's never having before appeared on screen. Lee Tracy played Hildy on Broadway and, although he had been in a few films, Hughes did not like him. It is interesting to note that he also did not like two other young actors then beginning their screen careers. He rejected James Cagney for Hildy because, "He's just a little runt," and Clark Gable because, "His ears stick out like a taxi with its doors open."

Milestone chose O'Brien after seeing him play the lead in *The Up and Up* on Broadway. He was even more impressed when O'Brien told him he had appeared on stage in *The Front Page.* Back in Hollywood, Milestone was able to convince Hughes, sight unseen, that O'Brien was their man. Hughes liked Milestone and never during the making of their three films together interfered with the director. When Milestone advised him that O'Brien, a Milwaukee Irishman then thirty years old, had a way with quick, glib dialogue, Hughes simply said, "Hire him."

Adolphe Menjou, Mary Brian, Pat O'Brien and the gold watch in *The Front Page*.

Before leaving New York, Pat O'Brien, far from confident about breaking into the movies with the lead in an important picture, went to see Lee Tracy because he felt embarrassed that the veteran actor, whom the New York critics had described as the perfect Walter Burns, had been so casually passed over by Hughes. Tracy seemed unconcerned and said that he probably could not have accepted the part anyway because he was under contract to producer Jed Harris and due to go into another play. Tracy then put O'Brien further at ease by advising him on the playing of the role and talking about his own experiences researching the newspaper business.

O'Brien struck up an immediate friendship with Louis Wolheim, whose ugly face masked a friendly nature. Wolheim helped him understand the mechanics of film acting, the business of following floor markings without making it apparent to the audience, and the difficult art of both being aware of the camera and ignoring it. Milestone rehearsed his cast for a week and at one point asked O'Brien how he had handled the scene on the stage in which the condemned man was placed in the roll-top desk. O'Brien caused a chill when he explained that he had never done the scene because he had played Walter Burns and not Hildy Johnson, and furthermore he had played him only in Cleveland. Milestone had hired him believing otherwise. For a moment the director was blank-faced. Then he smiled and said, "Let's go, Hildy."

Three weeks into production, the filming came to a jarring halt when Louis Wolheim collapsed. He had cancer and he died within days. Hughes and Milestone had the immediate problem of a replacement and mulled it over while the cast proceded with scenes not involving Burns. A week or so later Milestone announced to a surprised cast that Burns

69

would be played by Adolphe Menjou, which caused one of them to say, "He looks like a repainted Rolls-Royce." After a dozen years as a leading man in movies, Menjou's was a name with which to conjure, but his image was one of elegance and sophistication. Both on and off the scene he was a man of sartorial style, and the idea of him replacing Wolheim was like going from one end of the alphabet to the other. Be that as it may, Menjou proved splendid as Walter Burns. There was nothing in the script that said a conniving, unscrupulous editor could not also be dapper.

The Front Page not only turned out to be a winner with the critics and the public, but it became Hollywood's quintessential newspaper picture. Its pacing and its characters somehow convinced America and the world that this is how American newspapermen were—irreverent, cynical, curt with language and forever stomping in where angels fear to tread. Anything for a story. No matter how many protests came from the world of journalism, the image had been set by Hollywood, and very largely by *The Front Page.*

The image, however, began to fade once Hollywood had passed its Golden Age. Billy Wilder remade *The Front Page* in 1976, with Jack Lemmon as Hildy Johnson and Walter Matthau as Walter Burns, but despite the fine talent involved the film was a conspicuous flop. The Hecht-MacArthur stuff had finally become old-fashioned. The new version was a peculiar decision for Wilder to make, because there had been an excellent remake in 1940, when the authors agreed to alter the role of Hildy Johnson to a woman, played by Rosalind Russell, with Cary Grant as Burns, still conniving but much more charming. Charles Lederer scripted it and this time Ben Hecht played a direct part in the screen treatment. As *His Girl Friday*, splendidly directed by Howard Hawks, it became even more successful than the Hughes version.

Bucked up by having gained a winner with *The Front Page*, Howard Hughes now tried for something he believed would be even more potent at the box office. Films about gangsters, especially the Chicago breed which followed in the wake of Prohibition, were fairly common in Hollywood by 1931. When Hughes spoke of doing a gangster movie that would put others to shame, he was strongly advised not to do it. There had been something like one hundred movies on this subject since the advent of sound. Warner Bros. had had a major hit with Edward G. Robinson in *Little Caesar* and they were now in production with James Cagney in *The Public Enemy.* Warners, it seemed, was saying plenty about organized crime—what more could be said? Besides, the censors, both within the industry and without, were becoming concerned about this concentration of such an ugly aspect of American life. It was not doing much for the American image. All of which made Howard Hughes absolutely determined to make a movie about gangsters.

Hughes bought the rights to the novel *Scarface*, by Armitage Trail, and then asked Ben Hecht if he would be interested in turning it into a screenplay. Hecht shared the general view of Hughes as an eccentric, but he himself was something of an odd-ball when it came to dealing with

Scarface: Osgood Perkins, Vince Barnett, Paul Muni, Karen Morley and George Raft.

people. He had been through the hurly-burly life of a newspaper reporter and it had left him with a suspicious regard for humankind. He knew that Hughes was strange about money, that he never carried any and apparently never paid for anything with cash, so he laid down a stipulation before accepting Hughes's offer. Hecht wanted the sum of one thousand dollars a day for as long as he worked on the film and he wanted the sum paid at the end of each day. Hughes agreed and Hecht picked up his daily grand. That sum and those conditions did not, however, apply to the other writers who toiled on the *Scarface* screenplay: Seton I. Miller, John Lee Mahin, W. R. Burnett and Fred Pasley.

Hughes had only one director in mind for this picture—Howard Hawks, which came as a shock to Howard Hawks. They had had only one prior meeting and it was one Hawks told about with humorous flair. In late 1929 Hawks directed *The Dawn Patrol* for Warners, and since it was a film about First World War aviation he found himself using some of the stunt flyers Hughes was using on *Hell's Angels*, despite the fact that the flyers had signed contracts giving their employers exclusive rights to their services. Hawks claimed that one Sunday morning, while suffering from a hangover, he was awakened by a loud banging on his front door. He opened it to find Hughes in a state of rage, saying that not only was it unfair that Hawks was making a film on the same subject but that he had some of the same scenes, in particular scenes of fighter pilots being shot down and vomiting blood when hit in the chest and neck. Hawks allowed that this was true but claimed it was a natural reaction for any pilot being hit in the chest and neck. Hughes's demands that Hawks's scenes be deleted resulted in Hawks finally slamming the door in his face and going back to bed.

71

Some months later Hawks was perturbed to hear that Hughes was suing him because he had acquired interest in a play that Hughes had bought for filming. He was therefore more than a little surprised one day when he was playing golf at the Lakeside Country Club to be told that there was a phone call for him and that the call was from Hughes. Hughes said he would like to come out and play the course with him. Hawks angrily replied that he was in no mood to play with a man who was suing him. Hughes told Hawks to stand by the phone. Minutes later Hawks received a call from Hughes's lawyer telling him the case was being dropped, and to please wait for Mr. Hughes. The game that followed started with Hawks refusing all offers of employment at the first hole and showing keen interest in directing *Scarface* by the eighteenth. Hawks also claimed that he beat Hughes by shooting seventy-one, although never remembering what Hughes shot that day. Hughes liked to win, and on that particular day he may have won by losing.

The novel *Scarface* was a conventional account of the battles between the Chicago crime czars over bootleg liquor, and the main character was obviously based on Al Capone, even though the author denied it, just as Hughes and Hawks denied it once they began filming. Hecht was visited by a pair of Capone's henchmen while working on the script, because they had heard it was about their boss. Hecht convinced them that it had nothing to do with Capone, but that they were calling the film *Scarface* just to fool the public into thinking it might be about Capone. "That's part of the racket we call showmanship." The henchmen seemed to appreciate being let in on such inside matters. Next they asked if Howard Hughes had anything to do with it. Hecht replied that he had not, and added, with a wink, "He's just the sucker with the money."

Hawks became really interested in making the picture when he learned that Hecht would be the head writer, and he liked Hecht's idea that the story should be something like a modern account of the Borgias, an idea that would come to full blossoming many years later with *The Godfather.* With a good final script and an ample half-million-dollar budget, the problem was to find an actor to play the Caponish leading figure of Tony Camonte. Hughes was not interested in any of the Hollywood actors who had starred in gangster pictures. His film, of course, had to be different.

It was agent Al Rosen who suggested Paul Muni to Hughes. Rosen had seen Muni on Broadway and shared the New York opinion that he was an extraordinary actor. The Austrian-born Muni had cut his acting teeth in New York's Yiddish Art Theatre, in which his parents were prominent players, and by 1929 he was a leading actor on Broadway. Fox Pictures brought him to Hollywood that year and starred him in *The Valiant* and *Seven Faces*, but neither film was successful and Muni happily returned to New York, doubtful of any further involvement in the movies. When asked about his interest in *Scarface*, Muni flatly denied any, claiming that he was a non-physical, sedentary man by nature and hardly suited for anything so bizarre. It was his wife Bella, who handled his business affairs, who read the script and sensed that it would be an important property. Muni agreed to make a test in New York and

Scarface, with George Raft and C. Henry Gordon.

Paul Muni and Ann Dvorak in *Scarface*.

73

Paul Muni and Osgood Perkins in *Scarface*.

Hughes, who had never before even heard of him, accepted him for the role, with approval also coming from Hawks and Hecht.

The end result was a film that made Paul Muni a star and touched off a distinguished film career. And for an actor who claimed to be non-physical, it was a frighteningly physical performance, almost manic in its intensity. The critical consensus was that Muni dominated the film with his virile, vehement acting. Said *Variety*, "Muni, with a scar from his ear to his jaw, *is* Scarface. He's tough enough here to make Capone his errand boy. And convincing along with it, which has as much as anything else to do with the picture's merit."

Scarface begins as the powerful Johnny Lovo (Osgood Perkins) assassinates his main rival, Big Louis Costillo (Harry J. Vejar). Tony Camonte is chosen to do the killing, and he does it so well that Lovo promotes him to leadership status and promises him a cut of the profits. Camonte is soon a name to be reckoned with in the Chicago underworld, and as the money rolls in so does his ambition grow. Lovo warns him to cool his heels, especially in terms of Lovo's girlfriend Poppy (Karen Morley). He also warns him to stay out of a city ward run by a dangerous rival named O'Hara. Camonte ignores all warnings and opens up his own offices and hires an assistant, Angelo (Vince Barnett). Without consulting Lovo he instructs one of his top gunmen, Rinaldo (George Raft), to kill O'Hara.

Camonte's ego flourishes when he himself is the intended victim of an assassination. By now the machine gun has made its debut in Chicago, and Camonte is fascinated by it. He senses its power. When Lovo screams at him, "You murdering ape, you're going to take orders," Camonte picks up a machine gun and says, "This is the only thing that gives orders, Johnny. Get out of my way. I'm gonna spit." With that he gleefully splatters a wall with a torrent of bullets. The ape has found his ultimate tool. With three loads of gunmen he drives to the other ward and obliterates the remainder of O'Hara's gang.

Camonte becomes so cocky and so successful that Lovo decides to have something done about him. A plan to murder him goes awry and Camonte and Rinaldo turn up at Lovo's apartment. Lovo pleads for his life but Rinaldo coolly despatches him with a single bullet. Poppy moves in with Camonte, who now oozes wealth and influence. The only fly in this ointment is Camonte's overly protective regard for his beautiful sister Cesca (Ann Dvorak). Any man who comes near her is in trouble. Unfortunately she falls in love with Rinaldo, and he with her. On a vacation trip with Poppy, Camonte learns that Cesca and Rinaldo are living together; what he does not know is that they are married. He bursts into their apartment and without waiting for an explanation shoots Rinaldo. Afterwards the distraught Cesca calls the police, which eventually leads to Camonte's being trapped in his headquarters. When the police open up a barrage against him, the now contrite Cesca runs to his side but catches a bullet in the process and quickly dies. Camonte realizes he is now alone and is panic stricken. He babbles cowardly and as he runs from his building is gunned down. He dies writhing in the gutter.

Scarface ran into a barrage of censorship troubles, many of which were expected because the various censor boards across the country, abetted by newspaper editorials, had long deplored what they considered the licentious nature of Hollywood producers regarding sex and violence. With Howard Hughes making a film about crime the results were bound to be dazzling and shocking, and they were. Hughes kept his promise to keep off the set and not interfere, but he viewed each day's rushes and egged Hawks to make the picture as visually exciting as possible, with lots of machine gun fire, car chases and crashes.

Hollywood's self-censoring board—The Motion Picture Producers and Distributors of America, with Will Hays as chairman (the board was later better known as the Hays Office)—described the film as appalling when they screened it. They demanded cuts, some new material that would condemn gangsterism and a completely new ending. They felt that Camonte meeting his end in a blaze of gunfire was titillating and slightly glorifying. Hawks was defiant, but Hughes, realizing the extent of the opposition and the blacklisting that would come from releasing the film without an MPPDA Seal of Approval, agreed to trim a few of the more violent moments, to stick a little preachment in the middle and devise a new ending.

Paul Muni had left Hollywood after completing his scenes in the Fall of 1931 and, because of his appearance in a Broadway play, could not return for the new ending. Hawks used a double, filmed largely in shadows and long shots, to show Camonte being tried and proceeding to his death on the gallows. Then, because of the demands made by a variety of censors, the title was changed to *Scarface—The Shame of a Nation.* Hughes received a Seal of Approval but ran into a brick wall in New York when that city's Censorship Board banned the film. With that, the furious Hughes issued a statement to the press:

Scarface: Karen Morley and Paul Muni.

"It has become a serious threat to the freedom of honest expression in America when self-styled guardians of the public welfare, as personified by our censor boards, lend their aid and their influence to the abortive efforts of selfish and vicious interests to suppress a motion picture simply because it depicts the truth about conditions in the United States which have been front page news since the advent of Prohibition.

"I am convinced that the determined opposition to *Scarface* is actuated by political motives. The picture, as originally filmed eight months ago, has been enthusiastically praised by foremost authorities on crime and law enforcement and by leading screen reviewers. It seems to be the unanimous opinion of these authorities that *Scarface* is an honest and powerful indictment of gang rule in America and, as such, will be a tremendous factor in compelling our State and Federal governments to take more drastic action to rid the country of gangsterism."

Hughes' statement, as he shrewdly knew, created valuable publicity, in addition to winning him support in the press. *The New York Herald-Tribune* praised him as "the only Hollywood producer who has had the courage to come out and fight this censorship menace in the open. We wish him a smashing success." Hughes restored the cuts he had

75

made in the film and went back to his original ending. He released it in states that did not require censorship and the success of the picture built up interest elsewhere. He next filed a series of lawsuits against the censor boards of New York and those places that had blocked *Scarface*, and he won.

The reviews were uniformly high, and the public response was all Hughes could have hoped for. Those reviewers who felt that its commercial chances had been lessened by the delay in its release, and following such hits as *Little Caesar* and *The Public Enemy*, were proven wrong, as were those who described it as "the gangster picture to end all gangster pictures." That it was not. All through the 1930's Hollywood continued with a torrent of movies about rampant crime in America, especially in Chicago and New York. Warner Bros. virtually made this kind of film a house speciality, with the likes of Edward G. Robinson, James Cagney and Humphrey Bogart spending an unusual amount of their acting hours warding off the cops, sneering through prison bars and being shot to death on sidewalks. For all that, *Scarface* maintains a high listing in this genre. It has dated less than most of the others, and it retains its wallop. Aside from its subject matter it is a brilliantly crafted film, well paced by Hawks and illuminated by Muni's ferocious performance.

Howard Hawks claimed *Scarface* as his favorite among his own movies, and Howard Hughes was immensely proud of it. After a few years he locked it up in his vaults, from which it never emerged during the remainder of his life. Hughes refused many offers of distribution and he turned down requests from producers who wanted to buy the rights, including one who would have paid him two million dollars. Some years after his death his estate transacted a deal which resulted in the 1983 remake of *Scarface*, starring Al Pacino and altering the setting and period to contemporary Miami. The remake, produced in a time when censorship has become virtually minimal, shocked viewers with its graphic violence and a use of obscene language that might have lifted even the eyebrows of Al Capone. Be that as it may, it does not usurp the Hughes version either as a better film or a more persuasive treatment of the material. Hughes's *Scarface* deserves its place in film history.

Hughes's next proposed film project would have taken him back to aviation. By this time his interest in flying had become the predominant passion of his life. He made no secret of the fact that on the ground he felt awkward, especially when around people, but in the air he felt at home and at peace. The travail of making and launching *Scarface* had somewhat soured him on picture making and he reasoned that if he was to make another it should at least let him employ his enthusiasm for aviation. He announced his next film as *Zeppelin L-27*. The Zeppelin sequences in *Hell's Angels* continued to bring praise, besides which the doings of airships were in the news, especially the Atlantic crossings of the *Graf Zeppelin*. But getting a workable script and a reasonable budget together caused Hughes to abandon the idea. The Depression was in its depths and the people who ran his business interests bore down on him as hard as possible to avoid sinking vast amounts of money on a possible repetition of the financial chaos of *Hell's Angels*.

Howard Hughes now did something entirely unexpected, unreasonable and illogical—he turned his back on Hollywood and announced that he was devoting all his time to aviation. It was the middle of 1932 and he was twenty-six years of age. In view of all he had been through in his half-dozen years as a moviemaker it is difficult, as it was then, to think of him as a man of that age. Many young men had tackled Hollywood and failed, but this young man had tackled and won. He had made eleven movies and three of them had been enormously successful and would in fact become minor classics. It was an enviable track record. No one before or since has quit at such a point.

As the 1930's trudged by, it seemed less and less probable that Hughes would return to picture making. He left his comfortable Hollywood plateau and went on to a new way of life, although returning to the film capital for his social life and the courting of an endless parade of famous actresses, including Ida Lupino, Ginger Rogers, Bette Davis and Katharine Hepburn.

In the Spring of 1932 he founded Hughes Aircraft Company in Glendale, California, which relocated in Culver City nine years later, where it gradually grew into one of the most important and profitable aircraft production companies in the world. Hughes's personal triumph as an aviator began in the Spring of 1934 when he received a trophy at the All-American Air Meet in Miami, flying a Boeing pursuit plane he had bought from the Army and turned into a racer. In September of 1935, flying a sleek single-wing racer called the H-I, which he and his designers had devised, he set a new land speed record at Santa Ana, California, and the following January he set a new transcontinental speed record, flying from Los Angeles to Newark, New Jersey, in nine hours and twenty-seven minutes.

The aerial adventures of Howard Hughes throughout the 1930's made him a popular figure in the newspapers and on the airwaves. The ex-movie producer had become a real life hero. He seemed to be leading in the flesh the kind of life dealt with in Hollywood pictures, pictures in which the hero wins over improbable odds and does little else but succeed. In July of 1938 Hughes chalked up a success that even a scriptwriter might have hesitated to put on paper. With a re-modeled, twin-engined Lockheed 14 and a crew of four, Hughes flew all the way around the world and set a new record of three days, nineteen hours and twenty-eight minutes. On his return to New York, he and his men received a ticker-tape parade down Broadway, plus banquets and endless compliments. What aviator could ask for anything more? Howard Hughes could and did.

In May of 1939 Hughes acquired stock in Transcontinental and Western Airlines, which would later become Trans World Airlines. Now he was in commercial aviation transportation. In the fall of that year Hughes Aircraft began designs for new kinds of military aircraft; in the event of America's probable involvement in a war, his aircraft company would be of importance. By the end of 1939 there was no reason to believe that he would ever again have any interest in making motion pictures.

The George Hurrell portrait of Jane
Russell that helped launch her into stardom.

The Outlaw

The first person to learn that Howard Hughes was interested in getting back into film production was Russell Birdwell, whose reputation as a brilliantly imaginative publicist would expand quite a bit after his encounter with Hughes. It took place in Hollywood in late 1939, at a party following a showing of *Gone With the Wind*, for which Birdwell had devised and handled the long and florid publicity campaign. Birdwell recalled that Hughes, by then known as one of the worst and most carelessly dressed celebrities in America, was wearing an ill-fitting set of white tie and tails, and looked uncomfortably out of place. When he approached Birdwell and asked, "May I see you?" Birdwell, not knowing who he was, replied with a noncommital "later." It was Norma Shearer who told him that the man who had just walked sheepishly away was Howard Hughes.

Catching up with him a little later, Birdwell listened with some surprise as Hughes talked about making another movie and that he would need a publicist. Would Birdwell be interested? Birdwell, who could barely remember which had been the last Hughes movie and when, replied that he would indeed. Weeks later a messenger arrived to set up a meeting between the two men. It would be at Hughes's home and it would be at 1:30 in the morning. Birdwell may never before have held a meeting at that hour, but he was about to learn that his potential employer lacked a conventional regard for time and that meetings with him, and phone calls from him, very often took place in the middle of the night.

Birdwell was surprised and a little disappointed to learn that what

Jack Buetel as Billy the Kid, *The Outlaw* himself.

Hughes had in mind was a western with the title *Billy the Kid*. The story of the notorious western outlaw William H. Bonney was hardly new ground in Hollywood; King Vidor had directed a major accounting of this dubious westerner's life in 1930 with Johnny Mack Brown in the role and it had been titled *Billy the Kid*. The character had also turned up in numerous B westerns. This did not daunt Hughes, who explained that he was out to make an epic and that it would be different. It would, for example, be sexier than any western ever made. This intrigued Birdwell because westerns until that time were notable for being virtually sexless.

The meeting lasted until dawn and by then Birdwell was enthused about the concept of a super western that would break the old format. Hughes explained that for the part of Billy he wanted a complete unknown and that whoever played Billy's girlfriend should also be an unknown, but that she should be a girl who would make the same impact that Jean Harlow had made in *Hell's Angels*. This, Hughes explained, would be an essential factor in the success of the film. He had no intention of making an ordinary western. To this end he hired Howard Hawks as his director and Ben Hecht as his writer, but Hecht failed to come up with an outline that pleased Hughes and Hawks suggested a veteran scripter with whom he had worked several times, Jules Furthman. Furthman's ideas for plot, character and treatment were acceptable to Hughes.

Birdwell's initial publicity let the public and the industry know that Hughes was in need of a pair of wonderful youngsters to play the leads in *Billy the Kid*, and as a consequence Hughes's Hollywood headquarters at 7000 Romaine Street was swamped with photographs from agents and from hopefuls. Finding a young man for the title role proved to be fairly easy; agent Gummo Marx, the only one of the comedic brothers who never appeared in a movie, brought Jack Buetel in to meet Hughes. Buetel, then twenty-three, had recently arrived from Dallas, where his only acting experience had been a little theatre and in radio. Hughes immediately liked Buetel's baby-face handsomeness and signed him to a contract. It was the kind of good luck story that occasionally lightens the otherwise distressing truth about the hordes of youngsters who try to break into the movies.

The search for the girl was much more difficult. Much of the success of the picture would rest on the shoulders of the beauty finally chosen—as most clearly proved to be the case, but shoulders would not be much of a factor in the choice made by Hughes. The girl whom Hughes picked from a pile of photos was a nineteen-year-old named Ernestine Jane Geraldine Russell, who now looks back to 1940 and says, "I was a sex object before the term was invented. Having spent most of my teens skinny, I was just glad I'd filled out." It was, of course, the "filling out" that gives the otherwise lackluster *The Outlaw* its place in Hollywood history.

Jane Russell, born in Minnesota, had lived in Los Angeles since 1932, and after leaving school had taken a job as a chiropodist's receptionist. To supplement her income of ten dollars a week she posed as a model for

80

Jane Russell and Jack Buetel.

dresses and coats for Tom Kelley, the photographer who later struck it rich with his nude shots of the young Marilyn Monroe. With the encouragement of friends she joined the Max Reinhardt Theatrical Workshop in Hollywood and after half a year tried for some screen tests, none of which drew interest. It was agent Lewis Green who sent some of Kelley's photos of Russell to Hughes, from which came a test with Buetel—the scene being the rape in the barn.

Recalls Russell, "They gave me this peasant blouse to wear, and it was 'Janie, bend down and pick up those pails.' I did it, and the next thing I know, they're aiming the camera down to my navel." She turned to Howard Hawks for advice and he said, "You're a big girl. If you don't want to do something, say 'No' loud and clear. Nobody's going to look after you but you." The advice meant little when she saw the photos they had taken of her; she complained to Hughes, who gave her a cool reply, "That's the way to sell a picture." The statuesque, five-foot-seven girl with a thirty-eight-inch bust that looked as if it had been invented by Vargas could find no way to answer Hughes.

Shortly after production was set up in December of 1940, Hughes received a letter from Joseph Breen, who was in charge of issuing seals of approval at the Hays Office: "I see 'by the papers' as Mr. Dooley used to say, that you have begun shooting on your picture and it occurs to me that you ought to let us have a copy of your shooting script, with a view toward examining it, against the possibility that there may be some details in it, which will have to be deleted or changed in the finished picture." After reading the script Breen quickly got back to Hughes with several demands for changes in what he regarded as racy dialogue and situations, and added, "care must be taken to avoid sexual suggestiveness." Hughes promised to adhere to the wishes of the Hays Office and then proceeded to completely ignore them. He set up strict security around his production, advised his cast and crew not to talk about the film and refused his actors the usual perogative of viewing the daily rushes.

Not long after the picture started filming, MGM put one of their own projects before the camera. It's title—*Billy the Kid*, with Robert Taylor in the role. Hughes phoned Louis B. Mayer to complain. Mayer said he was sympathetic but he certainly had every right to remake the studio's 1930 version; perhaps Mr. Hughes might consider doing another kind of film or at least changing the title. Nothing on earth would have convinced the dogged Hughes to change his mind about anything once that mind was set, but he obviously needed another title. Someone among his cohorts suggested *The Outlaw*, which in view of the film's disregard for Hollywood propriety seemed an appropriate choice. In spite of his annoyance at the time, the change of title proved providential for a movie that would forever change the western as a form and, whether Hughes intended it or not, cause upheavals in the American attitude toward sex on the screen.

Basically *The Outlaw* is a four-character screenplay. In addition to Billy and his girlfriend Rio, the others are the flamboyant, crooked Doc Halliday and Sheriff Pat Garrett, the former played by Walter Huston and the latter by Thomas Mitchell. The hiring of these two respected veterans was a boon to the film, since the acting talents of the two young leads proved almost painfully inadequate. It would have taken a patient director to draw performances from Buetel and Russell. Instead they were subjected to the part-time, long-winded leadership of Howard Hughes. After a few weeks of shooting, Howard Hawks gave up and suggested to Hughes that he himself take over the direction. During the making of *Scarface* Hughes had respectfully kept his distance. Now he seemed a different man, much more demanding, more willful, fussier and less tolerant of other opinions. Perhaps the eight years of success in aviation had given him more confidence in his abilities as a commanding officer. Whatever it was, it made this second plateau of his film career considerably more tortuous then the first.

Shooting began on *The Outlaw* on a handsome location in Arizona, some eighty miles east of Flagstaff. Hughes had the daily rushes flown to him each night and immediately called Hawks after viewing them, no matter what the hour. Hughes had wisely hired one of Hollywood's most esteemed cameramen, Gregg Toland, who had just added to his laurels with *Citizen Kane*, but there was something about the photography that bothered Hughes—no clouds. The old *Hell's Angels problem* was bedevilling Hughes again. He told Hawks to take his time, to wait for clouds, money was no object. After a few weeks of spending time with a cast and crew of over two hundred people on a distant location and getting very little footage, Hawks asked to see Hughes. He explained that he had an

Thomas Mitchell and Walter Huston, the bored veterans of *The Outlaw.*

offer from Warners to direct an obviously important picture, *Sergeant York* with Gary Cooper, and that he could not spend months working on this western. Hughes was sympathetic and Hawks was regretful but it is likely that both men were relieved to be free of each other. With Hawks's departure Hughes ordered the entire company back to Los Angeles, and the whole eight-car train Hughes had hired was shunted back in short order.

In its first release *The Outlaw* ran one minute over two hours, an unusually long time for a 1940's film and especially so for a western with so slight a story. It begins with Billy admitting to Doc that he stole his horse and with the sheriff wanting to lock the young renegade in jail. Doc asks him not to because he and Billy are actually friends. Doc's sultry girlfriend Rio then tries to kill Billy in revenge for his killing of her brother, but Billy tells her it was in self-defense. He then forcibly makes love to her in a barn—a virtual rape, but one in which she barely gets mussed up. Sheriff Pat hires a bunch of gunmen to shoot Billy but he outwits and outdraws them. He is, however, wounded in the fight and makes his way to the house where Doc lives with Rio. Doc is away and she somewhat begrudgingly decides to look after him, which includes climbing into bed with the delirious, shivering Billy to keep him warm. While he is still in delirium, Rio brings in a priest to marry them (a piece of business added to the completed film at the request of the Hays Office).

When Doc returns he is furious to find Billy with Rio, but Billy is confused because he remembers very little. Both men agree that horses are really of more value than women anyway and take off to seek their fortune together. The offended Rio drains their canteens of water and

Howard Hughes on the set of *The Outlaw*, with a puzzled Jack Buetel leaning against the wall.

fills them with sand, which causes Billy to drag her out to the open desert and leave her there. The pursuing sheriff catches up with Billy and Doc, captures them but returns their guns when they are attacked by Indians. They outmaneuver the Indians and escape, and then return to town, with the sheriff still following, intent on bringing the two outlaws to justice. Finally the sheriff shoots and mortally wounds Doc, but Billy gets the drop on the sheriff and ties him up. Rio and Billy, now realizing their love, ride off into the sunset as Doc is buried in a grave on which the tombstone bears the name of William H. Bonney, Billy the Kid. With the world believing him dead, perhaps he will be able to live in peace. Thus ends this fable invented by scenarist Joel Furthman and producer-director Howard Hughes.

The Outlaw finished shooting on February 7, 1941. It had provided employment for a large number of people for more than a year, but it had bored and exhausted most of them. No film had ever before been made under such circumstances. Hughes had spent most of his time and energies at his aircraft plant, particularly on developing military aircraft with the object of winning government contracts, and most of his involvement with the film was done in the evening, often way into the night. For Russell and Buetel it might have been boring, but they were at least breaking into the movies with leading roles in a big picture. But for Walter Huston and Thomas Mitchell the experience was often humiliating. Both threatened to quit on several occasions, and the hot-tempered Mitchell frequently stormed at Hughes, questioning his ability and his sanity as Hughes demanded take after take after take. At one point Mitchell referred to it as "a bastard of a film."

It was obvious to all who were making the picture that Hughes intended to capitalize on Jane Russell's bust. He instructed Toland to photograph it to advantage, and in one scene where she was writhing while tied between two stakes he was especially concerned about the thrust of her breasts. He thereupon sat down and designed a brassiere for her, employing, he claimed, engineering principles. This incident has assumed legendary proportions over the years, but Russell claims she never actually wore it: "Howard was trying to invent the seamless bra of today. It was a brilliant idea but too uncomfortable."

When the Hay Office viewed the picture, the results were much as Hughes had expected, but more so. Joseph Breen wrote to Hughes outlining all the many objections, none of which were quite as strongly voiced as those Breen expressed in a letter to Hays: "In my more than ten years of critical examination of motion pictures I have never seen anything quite so unacceptable as the shots of the breasts of the character Rio. Throughout almost half the picture the girl's breasts, which are large and prominent, are shockingly uncovered." Breen also implied that this film might possibly trigger an increasingly liberal attitude toward female nudity in movies. If Breen were alive today he would have the right to look a little self-satisfied.

By the film standards of the 1980's *The Outlaw* is tepid stuff. The rape in the barn looks like a frolic in which the girl's clothes are barely disturbed and, although the film displays Russell's bust to the maximum in low cut blouses, she is never even partly nude. Aside from the accent of flesh, the censors and critics were offended by the script's attitude towards regard for the girl—an attitude that today would be even more unacceptable—which makes her appear a secondary human. Doc and Billy banter about her in terms of her worth compared to a horse, and after the incident of Billy and Rio having slept together, Doc rejects her: "I don't want her now. Cattle don't graze after sheep."

Hughes decided to fight the Hays Office. His lawyers placed an appeal with the Motion Picture Association of America and Hughes presented evidence that female breasts had always been an intriguing factor in movies, whereupon he displayed photos of some of Hollywood's more generously endowed beauties. After a great deal of protracted arguments Hughes agreed to make a number of minor cuts and changes in his film, and he was granted a Seal of Approval on March 23, 1941. Other producers might have launched the film the next day. Not Hughes. He and the cunning Russell Birdwell held the film back for almost two years, during which time Birdwell worked a brilliant publicity campaign, much of it involving Jane Russell.

The campaign began with Birdwell contracting the masterly photographer George Hurrell to shoot some studies of Russell, attired in a low-cut blouse and sprawling in a haystack. *Life* took immediate advantage of the beautiful shots, as did others, and Russell was soon a major magazine cover girl. With Birdwell's skill and the wholehearted enthusiasm of servicemen everywhere, Russell became one of the favorite pin-up girls of the Second World War, and was hailed as a movie star without ever having been seen in a movie.

Hughes explaining to the hot-tempered Thomas Mitchell what it is he wants.

85

The decision was made to launch *The Outlaw* at the Geary Theatre in San Francisco on February 5, 1943. Birdwell arranged for almost the entire press corps of Hollywood to be flown to the premiere. The reaction was more than he had anticipated; titters developed into guffaws as the reporters and reviewers squirmed through the long picture. Perhaps the kindest reaction was that of *Variety*, which decided not to review it. The Catholic Legion of Decency banned *The Outlaw* and many people phoned newspapers and theatres complaining about the lewdness of the film. One of the people who made a great number of calls was Russell Birdwell, who assumed a variety of names as he sniffed in disgust at the blatant exploitation of Jane Russell. It was also Birdwell who supervised the startling billboards, which featured only the charms of Jane, with the slogan, "How'd you like to tussle with Russell?"

The Outlaw played throughout America for ten weeks, weathering storms of controversy, much of it whipped up by Birdwell, and during the time it brought Hughes a large profit on his investment. Since he was by this time in his life calculated to be worth between twenty and thirty million dollars, it was hardly his main concern, but in his mind it did justify the making of the movie. How much of the success of *The Outlaw* is attributable to Russell Birdwell is not hard to figure out.

The advertising for *The Outlaw* was more salacious than the film itself, and it did not go uncriticized within the Hollywood community. Darryl F. Zanuck complained that Birdwell's publicity tactics were disgraceful, particularly his sending up of sky writers to inscribe the name of the film over Los Angeles, followed by two circles with dots in the middle. Comedians made much of Jane Russell's possessing two major reasons for her claim to fame. Russell herself became resentful, especially since her salary at the time of the 1943 release was still $75.00 a week. She had done nothing for two years except be involved with *The Outlaw*, which included long periods of inactivity, and in April of 1943 she walked out on Hughes and eloped with her high school sweetheart, football star Bob Waterfield. Hughes placed her on suspension, which lasted for two years. Waterfield went into the Army and Jane worked for War Bond drives under her married name. They returned to California in late 1945 when Waterfield left the Army, and Hughes reinstated Russell when she returned to Hollywood. He had no plans for movies at that time and loaned her to producer Hunt Stromberg to co-star with Louis Hayward in *Young Widow*, which was released in 1946. Critics noted that her acting ability had not improved, but she did appear to be more at ease. She was certainly more mature than the naïve, innocent youngster who first stepped before the cameras to test for the part of Rio.

After enjoying ten good weeks with *The Outlaw*, Hughes withdrew the picture. He never explained why, but it is a fair assumption that he believed its languishing on the shelf for another few years could do nothing but increase its notoriety. But an even bigger reason was his role as a wartime aircraft manufacturer, which among things required competing with companies like Lockheed and Douglas for government contracts. With Hughes it went beyond mere competition; he was an

Russell as the sultry but well attired Rio, with Joseph Sawyer and Mimi Aguglia.

aviation idealist who thought in terms of radically different kinds of aircraft and who was constantly experimenting with one concept or another.

Hughes reissued *The Outlaw* in 1946, when it ran into more censorial problems and more profit. This time the Motion Picture Association of America decided to withdraw the Seal of Approval they had granted three years previously, which was something they had never done before. This caused Hughes to sue the MPAA, which was also something that had not been done before. It sent shivers through Hollywood, which was already growing paranoid over the government's intention to invoke the anti-trust laws and separate the film studios from their ownership of chains of theatres. The Hays Office was a body not essentially concerned with morality; its primary purpose was self-government within the industry, in order to protect Hollywood from the hordes of censors across America. Now it seemed as if Howard Hughes was shaking the whole structure.

Despite the powerful tactics of Hughes's lawyers they were not able to sway the judges, and Hughes had to be satified with his film playing in those houses that were willing to take it minus a Seal of Approval. What with the legendary status of *The Outlaw* and the new wave of publicity, those houses had no reason to regret showing the film. After some months of these showings Hughes backed down in his battle with the MPAA and agreed to the cuts they suggested. This got him back his Seal of Approval and ample bookings from theatres eager to show it. Even the Legion of Decency altered their condemnation and gave the film a B rating, one that branded it "morally objectionable in part." By this time it hardly mattered. *The Outlaw* may have been trounced by

87

every critic in every city in the United States and the British Commonwealth but it had made millions of dollars profit and it had kept the name Howard Hughes glaringly alive. The man who owned the name may have become increasingly shy and withdrawn, but he was extremely concerned with that name being known and respected.

With his unusual methods, bizarre personal behavior and fantastic publicity Hughes created in *The Outlaw* a film which deserves little of its almost milestone status in film annals. It most certainly would not have created much furore without its young leading lady, who shares the general opinion that it is an overrated and largely dull piece of film. "I thought the picture was ghastly and that I looked like a wooden dummy. I don't know how I ever got another part. All that fuss over my, well, physicality was very embarrassing." On the other hand, it is that picture which gives Russell a place in Hollywood history and a career that might not otherwise have materialized. In that regard she was luckier than Jack Buetel; he was kept under contract by Hughes for seven years, but it was not until 1951, a decade after he started *The Outlaw*, that he appeared in another film, the western *Best of the Badman*. He made four more westerns before drifting out of the picture business in 1959 and finding a new career in the business world.

Film historians cannot completely disregard *The Outlaw*. In his book *The Face on the Cutting Room Floor*, Murray Schumach makes the point that regardless of Hughes's motives, he did in fact bring some honesty into Hollywood's hypocritical handling of sex. "He made the American public laugh a little at its own prudery about the female breasts. If ever a cinematic Rabelais emerges from Hollywood, he will be indebted to this unusual industrialist." There have been many Rabelaisian film makers in recent times, but one wonders how much they appreciate the breakthrough forced by Hughes, who, at a time when married couples on the screen could only cohabit in twin beds, actually showed a voluptuous young lady getting into bed with a man. And in terms of the western as a film genre, those formerly sexually arid ranges breathed a little heavier thanks to Hughes.

Much had happened to Howard Hughes during the years *The Outlaw* was in production and in contention. As a wartime industrialist he had assumed considerable importance with his aircraft company, while at the same time Hughes Tool Company had steadily grown. In November of 1942 he joined forces with shipbuilder Henry J. Kaiser and won a government contract to build three huge flying boats, of which only one would ever be completed, the famed Spruce Goose. In May of the following year he crashed into Lake Mead, Nevada, in a Sikorsky S-43; he survived with slight injuries but two men with him died. Not long before that he had been involved in a minor traffic accident, in which his head was cut and bruised. And in late 1943 Hughes suffered his first nervous breakdown.

The strain of making *The Outlaw* was minimal compared to being a wartime manufacturer and aircraft designer. The government contract to produce flying boats was eventually cancelled because it was impossi-

The Geary Theatre, San Francisco, on the opening night of *The Outlaw,* February 5, 1943.

ble to produce the mammoth planes in time for use in the war, and other contracts for the manufacture of military reconnaissance planes also ended up cancelled. The failures rankled Hughes much more than his many successes. It caused him to become ever more suspicious of humankind, and it exacerbated his hypochondria. He nonetheless possessed amazing luck. Hughes had survived a number of air crashes, and on July 7, 1946, he survived one which was against all odds. He was test piloting his magnificently designed XF-11 and, while flying over Los Angeles, the engines malfunctioned, causing the plane to spin out of control. Hughes crashed between two houses on North Linden Drive in posh Beverly Hills. The plane was smashed to pieces as it exploded and burned. He was pulled from the wreck and rushed to the hospital, where it was doubted he would live. His chest was crushed, a lung had collapsed, seven ribs were broken, his head was lacerated and he was cut and burned all over. Incredibly he recovered within a month and was released from the hospital on August 12. Even more incredibly he was behind the controls of a plane and flying on September 9. To the world it seemed as if Howard Hughes was back to being his old self, but only a few knew that in order to tolerate his pain he had become addicted to codeine. He would stay addicted to it until the end. After that crash, he was on the road to being someone decidedly other than his old self.

7

Diddlebock and Faith

Harold Lloyd in *Mad Wednesday.*

Why Howard Hughes chose to involve himself further in the motion picture business is difficult to understand. The reasons were known only to him, and he was not a man who felt moved to explain anything he did. He was also not a man who gave up on anything. As a youngster he had set himself certain goals—to be successful in aviation, in the movie business and as a golfer. The last he did finally give up on, most probably because of declining health after the age of fifty. As a pilot there had been no doubt about his success—in fact, he had assumed the rank of hero in that sphere—and as a film producer he had done very well for himself. *The Outlaw* may not have been a good motion picture, but through sheer tenacity he had made it one of the most famous movies ever.

The Outlaw brought Hughes considerable profits when he re-released it in 1946. After a year or so he withdrew it and put it back in the closet, from which it did not emerge again until 1950. He was then in command of RKO Studios and he sold it to the company, along with two other pictures he had produced independently before taking over RKO in 1948—*The Sin of Harold Diddlebock*, retitled *Mad Wednesday* when reissued, and *Vendetta*. These two films form the least-known portion of Hughes's life as a Hollywood producer. The first was made in cooperation with the brilliant writer-director Preston Sturges and brought the long retired Harold Lloyd back to the screen, and the second was a

90

Harold Lloyd and Jimmy Conlin in *Mad Wednesday.*

showcase for an actress Hughes first met when she was fifteen—Faith Domergue.

Neither film was successful, and since they were made in the immediate postwar period, at a time when Hughes was beset with problems stemming from his work as an aircraft manufacturer, it would have been understandable if he had simply ended this phase of his activities. He certainly had more serious things on his mind, starting with his compulsive need to recover from his crash of July 7, 1946, and to build a new model of the XF-11 and to prove it a success. This he did on April 5, 1947. Four months later he testified before the Senate War Investigating Committee, which had probed into his work as a defense contractor. Hughes had made enemies in the fiercely competitive war years and he had not been nearly as successful as he had hoped. Hughes Aircraft had not become the giant he had planned—that would come later in the Space Age. Building the massive flying boat, which became known as the Spruce Goose because of its mostly wooden construction, had taken far too long to be of use in the war, but all charges that it was not airworthy were dispelled when Hughes personally took it for its one and only flight, in Long Beach Harbor, on November 2, 1947. On the face of it, there was no need for such a man to bother himself with the picture business.

The old adage about life beginning at forty does not apply to Howard Hughes. He was forty when he crashed his XF-11 and, although he made a recovery that almost defied medical science, he seemed after that to be a much older and sadder man. One of the few people who could get an interview from him at that time was columnist Earl Wilson,

91

Mad Wednesday: Jimmy Conlin, Frank Moran, Harold Lloyd and Torben Meyer.

who expressed the opinion that the recovery was miraculous. Hughes raised his eyebrows, "I guess it was, but I consider that I was very unlucky to have had that accident in the first place. It was caused by a freak mechanical failure that never should have occurred. It has never happened before, and the chances are that it will never happen again. I feel all right. I lost 35 pounds and haven't gained it back. But I hope to, soon. I burned my left hand pretty badly tearing back the lucite canopy of the plane getting out. I'll never be able to straighten two of my fingers. That'll be the only permanent injury." Hughes was, of course, being optimistic. He may have recovered from the physical injuries, but his strangely introverted, withdrawn, doggedly independent personality seemed to become more firmly set from then onwards.

Another man of doggedly independent nature was writer-director-producer Preston Sturges. Hughes was among the many who admired Sturges's marvelous, unusual, satiric movies. Sturges had been a successful screen writer all through the 1930's but in 1940 he managed to persuade Paramount to let him direct his satire on American politics titled *The Great McGinty*, which won him an Oscar for best screenplay. With that Sturges took off like a rocket. Over the next four years came *Christmas in July, The Lady Eve, Sullivan's Travels, The Palm Beach Story, The Miracle of Morgan's Creek*, and *Hail the Conquering Hero*. Among writer-directors, Sturges was himself a conquering hero. When his Paramount contract came up for renewal in 1944, complete with a guarantee of one million dollars, he refused it. MGM made him an even better offer and he refused that, too. Preston Sturges wanted to be independent.

Hughes and Sturges became friends during the early Thirties. They were drawn to each other and for good reasons. Both were eccentrics, although Sturges was far more genial. Both were in a sense Renaissance men; no matter what they did they wanted to do everything. In the case of Sturges, he wanted to direct and produce his own screenplays, cast them and edit them. In short he was a One Man Band, and nobody admired that kind of man more than Howard Hughes.

Sturges had been born into a wealthy family and in 1947 he was named by the Treasury Department as one of the highest paid men in the land. He owned two yachts, which made him one-up on Hughes, a successful playhouse-restaurant in Hollywood known as The Players, a large mansion that was overflowing with his many inventions, and he owned and operated a factory, Sturges Engineering Company, which among other things produced Diesel engines during the war. If his screenplays tended to mock the frantic American hunger for success, it must be assumed that he spent a little time looking in the mirror. Preston Sturges was many-sided. He was also enigmatic and contradictory. How would such a man be able to work with Howard Hughes?

One of the reasons that Sturges did not renew his Paramount contract is that Hughes had made a suggestion to him—that they form a motion picture company together. In late 1944 they registered California Pictures Corporation, with Hughes owning the controlling shares. It was agreed that their first venture was to be *The Sin of Harold Diddlebock*, which Sturges had written with Harold Lloyd in mind. Lloyd had been, along with Charlie Chaplin and Buster Keaton, one of the three greatest comedians of the silent screen. Lloyd made a few sound movies, but after *Professor Beware* in 1938 he decided to retire. Unlike many another silent movie comic, he was a shrewd businessman and by 1938 was wealthy. He thereafter supervised various business interests, including many charities, and he devoted much time to the Shriners. He lived on one of the most splendid estates in Beverly Hills, in a house comedian Ed Wynn once referred to as having only thirty-six rooms, "but it's home to Harold." He had no need to subject himself to the labors of film making, but Sturges came to him with a script he could hardly refuse, since it was a virtual homage to Lloyd. With added persuasion by Hughes, who both knew and admired Lloyd, the great comic was inveigled out of his comfortable retirement.

California Pictures set up offices and rented studio space at the Samuel Goldwyn Studios in Hollywood, which was then the center of activity for most of the independent film producers, most of whom released through United Artists, whose headquarters were also at the Goldwyn Studios. It was agreed that UA would be the distributors for California Pictures. Filming on *The Sin of Harold Diddlebock* began in late 1945 and was completed by the following spring. When the company had been established a year previously, Hughes had called a press conference and announced, "I want to make one thing clear—I can't devote any time whatsoever to the motion picture business until the war is over. Sturges is the one man in whom I have complete confidence. I

93

On the set of *Mad Wednesday*, with visiting pianist José Iturbi, Frances Ramsden, Jimmy Conlin, Harold Lloyd, director Preston Sturges and Percy Helton.

am happy to turn over to him the full control and direction of all my motion picture activities." Although the words must have fallen pleasingly on the ears of Preston Sturges, there were probably a few reporters present who were left with a lingering doubt or two.

Throughout the shooting of *Diddlebock*, Hughes did in fact keep out of Sturges's way. With a generous budget of two million dollars Sturges was able to make the film as he wished, after which he edited it to what he considered a trim ninety minutes. He had the inspired idea of making his opening sequence the closing sequence of Lloyd's classic 1925 comedy *The Freshman*, which was the story of a genial, bumbling college boy who yearned to be popular and finally made the grade by winning an important football game. Sturges took those exciting and hilarious final moments and spliced in shots of a business tycoon, E. J. Waggleberry (Raymond Walburn) cheering from the stands. He afterwards offers Harold a job in his company, explaining that it is a job at the bottom of the ladder in order to give him the opportunity to climb that ladder. Says Waggleberry, in a line typical of Sturges's acid humor, "How I envy you—my father, unfortunately, left me the business."

Harold Diddlebock's joyful start sadly leads to nowhere. Twenty years flash by and Harold is still at the bottom of the ladder. Now he is a shabby, dispirited clerk, and Waggleberry terminates his services, saying, "You not only make the same mistakes year after year, you don't even change your apologies." Harold is given a gold watch in recognition of his twenty years and he departs, although not until he has said goodbye to office girl Miss Otis (Frances Ramsden), who is but the most recent in the long line of office girls with whom Harold has been in love during his years with Waggleberry.

Soon after leaving Waggleberry's employ Harold meets an elfin-like hustler named Wormsy (Jimmy Conlin), who injects some excitement into Harold's life, mostly by getting him drunk and persuading him to part with his life's savings. The former teetotaler goes delightfully berserk under the influence of alcohol. He invests in a glaring plaid suit and proceeds to the racetrack, where he slaps down a one thousand dollar bet on a longshot, which comes in at fifteen-to-one. When he wakes up on Thursday morning and realizes he has no recollection of Wednesday, a day of gaiety and madness in which he apparently bought a circus. Now comes the problem of what to do with it. He descends on the place where money is best represented—Wall Street—and in order to get attention he takes with him a lion on a leash. During one of the visits to a string of bankers, the lion gets loose, causing Harold, Wormsy and a banker to seek escape by climbing out the window of a skyscraper and onto a ledge hundreds of feet above the sidewalks—and thereby giving Harold Lloyd and Preston Sturges a chance to revive the breathtaking comic stunts that played such a vital part in many of the classic Lloyd comedies, particularly *Safety Last* (1923).

After dangling for a frantic, extended period from the side of the skyscraper, Harold is arrested and jailed. Miss Otis bails him out and informs him, to his delight, that one of the things he did during his lost

95

Faith Domergue.

Wednesday was to marry her. Next come all the bankers, now aware of the publicity and bidding with each other to own the circus. But the Ringling Brothers, keen to eliminate competition, make the best offer and hand Harold a check for $175,000. Then Waggleberry enters to offer Harold a partnership in the firm and all is well.

The Sin of Harold Diddlebock was not released for almost a year. Harold Lloyd was not pleased with it or the way it had been made. Most of his finest films were made for his own company and he was used to calling the shots. The euphoria that triggered the project and the good feelings and mutual admiration between the comedian and the writer-director-producer gradually turned cool, as they did with Hughes when he saw the results. These were three men used to doing things their own way, and shortly after the film started shooting it was apparent that the ways of Sturges and Lloyd varied. At first it was agreed that they would shoot scenes two ways in order to compare results, but this became tedious and Lloyd finally settled for doing the film according to Sturges's dictates. Sturges appeared well satisfied with his picture, but when it was released in February of 1946 it met with only mild response from the critics and almost apathy on the part of the public.

After a few months Hughes did what he had done before with dubious pictures—he withdrew *Diddlebock* and put it on the shelf. Two years later Hughes pulled it off the shelf and sat down to edit it, but not in the company of Sturges, who had left California Pictures. He trimmed a dozen minutes out of it, including one whole sequence that featured Rudy Vallee as a banker, put back a few bits from outtakes, and gave it the more arresting title *Mad Wednesday*, which he released in 1950 through RKO. For Sturges it was the first break in the unusual run of

Vendetta: Peter Coe (in the dock) and Faith Domergue.

good luck he had enjoyed since 1940. Sturges purists claim that his film was butchered, but those who have seen both versions favor the tighter, faster-paced Hughes version, even though it too found no real success. On the other hand, those who appreciate the work of Harold Lloyd are left wondering what the film might have been had it been left in his hands. Critics at the time commented that it was a strange picture, with some brilliant moments, especially the skyscraper sequence, interspersed by plodding, unfunny stretches. But if nothing else, *Mad Wednesday* stands as the last, and partly amusing, film of a giant of American film comedy.

Preston Sturges doubtless had a number of his own scripts in mind to put into production after *Diddlebock*, but Hughes, now that he had a little more time than previously to devote to the course of California Pictures, also had some of his own ideas as to what should be made next. He had been looking around for something in which to star young Faith Domergue, whom he had had under contract for two years. Someone brought to his attention the gothic tale *Colomba* by Prosper Mérimée, and he asked Sturges to do a screen treatment. Since it was a yarn about revenge in nineteenth-century Corsica, Sturges decided on the more dramatic title *Vendetta.*

Faith Domergue came to Hughes's attention when they were both guests at a boating party in Balboa in 1940. Hughes appeared to be almost transfixed by this young girl with black hair and dark blue eyes. She had been born in New Orleans of French and Spanish parents and was such an arrestingly beautiful girl that Warners had put her under contract only a few weeks previously. Since she was only fifteen they were prepared to spend a couple of years developing her talents, which

97

included correcting a lisp, and supporting her education. They had no chance to do anything because the day after Hughes met her he purchased her contract from Warners. Any hope on her part that this impetuous man was about to rush her into pictures gradually dissolved, and it was not until the summer of 1947 that Faith Domergue started to learn the lines for *Vendetta*. In all that time she had received a weekly wage, attained a good education, perfected her diction and waited to be called by Hughes. In early 1947 she also found time to marry bandleader Teddy Stauffer in Acapulco, but that marriage ended in divorce in October of that year, after which she immediately married Argentinian film director Hugo Fregonese. By the time her first movie, *Vendetta*, was released in 1950, she was already the mother of a daughter.

Preston Sturges began production on *Vendetta* during the summer of 1946, when Hughes was still in the hospital. Prior to the air crash Hughes had agreed with Sturges to hire the eminent German director Max Ophuls to shoot from a Sturges script, with Sturges in charge of production. Ophuls was in Hollywood, having just directed Douglas Fairbanks, Jr., in the swashbuckler *The Exile*, and it was decided that his cultured touch was right for the costumed melodramatics of *Vendetta*. Sturges spent one million dollars during the first six weeks of filming, after which the barely recovered Hughes came to the studio to look at the results. He liked nothing of what he saw and told Sturges to get rid of Ophuls and to start re-doing the film with himself as director. Hughes especially disliked the unimaginative way Ophuls had photographed the lovely Domergue and instructed Sturges that this was to be a primary consideration from that point onward.

Sturges's speciality had always been comedy of the quickly paced, bitingly witty kind, and the dark, humorless situations of *Vendetta* suited his style not at all, which is why he did not choose to direct it in the first place. He could muster up no enthusiasm for it and, unusual for such an active man, spent days shooting very little footage, most of which he decided not to print. When Hughes returned to the studio some weeks later he was furious that so little had been done, and he battled with his partner. Probably to Sturges's relief, California Pictures Corporation was thereupon dissolved. Sturges was gentlemanly in commenting on the break up: "Interruptions have been frequent in Mr. Hughes's productions. But he has never made a failure. Both he and I are doers, and neither of us is content to sit by and watch someone else work. I became an independent producer to get away from supervision. When Mr. Hughes made suggestions with which I disagreed, as he has a perfect right to do, I rejected them. When I rejected the last one, he remembered that he had an option to take control of the company and he took over. So I left."

In leaving Hughes and making his settlements Sturges forfeited all rights to *The Sin of Harold Diddlebock* and whatever work he had put into *Vendetta*, but by the time that picture was completed there was barely a trace of his work left. Hughes brought in the veteran W. R. Burnett to re-write the script and Stuart Heisler to take over the

Vendetta, with George Dolenz and Faith Domergue.

direction, but he did not like the way Heisler handled the material and he fired him. While deciding on another director, Hughes did a few scenes himself before making his final choice, Mel Ferrer, who was a strange choice in view of the fact that the then thirty-year-old actor had never before directed a film. Some critics were cruel enough to point out that it was obvious that he had not.

Unfortunately, Preston Sturges's career never truly got back on the track. After leaving Hughes he went to 20th Century-Fox to make *Unfaithfully Yours*, a witty treatment of supposed infidelity which led his fans to believe he was assuming his former stature as a film satirist, but it was followed by the mediocre *The Beautiful Blonde From Bashful Bend* (1949), and this ended his Hollywood career. He made only one more film, in Paris in 1956, *Les Carnets du Major Thompson*, which was released in America as *The French They Are a Funny Race*, an almost total flop. He died in 1959, aged sixty-one, still full of ideas but with hardly any of his fortune left. After their break-up he and Hughes had never seen or spoken to each other again. The only detectable bitterness on the part of Sturges may be found in *Unfaithfully Yours*, when Hugo, the character played by Lionel Stander, makes a reference to the stuffed-shirt brother-in-law (Rudy Vallee) of Sir Alfred De Carter (Rex Harrison) as owning one hundred million dollars. Sir Alfred haughtily replies that he has a few million himself. Hugo snaps back, "You ain't got a hundred million. It's that last zither that cooks the goose."

The filming of *Vendetta* went on and on and on. Each director had a different concept and wanted to refilm previous scenes and between directors there were long stretches in which the cast and crew did

99

nothing for weeks on end, but always in the expectation that Hughes would turn up to give them guidance. He rarely did because he had business in other directions. One of the actors who became greatly concerned about his career at this juncture was leading man George Dolenz, a handsome Yugoslav who had played a string of second leads since arriving in Hollywood in 1941. *Vendetta* gave him his first opportunity as a lead but it kept him off the screen for three years, after which he went back to being a supporting player. Dolenz met Hughes one evening in a Hollywood night club. Despite having been on the payroll for two years, he had never been introduced to Hughes. At this meeting Dolenz introduced himself, at which Hughes looked blank. The actor then explained he was playing the leading man in *Vendetta*, the part of Orso. At this Hughes smiled and thanked him for his work and for his patience. He left the puzzled Dolenz with these words, "Believe in me. Believe in the picture. Believe in the company." It was the only conversation the two men ever had.

In *Vendetta*, a murky tale that called for massive amounts of fake fog swirling around the sets, interspliced with establishing shots of Corsica, Orso is the older brother of Colomba (Domergue). He is called back from his military life in France and this fiery-blooded girl convinces him that they must avenge the murder of their father. The murderers are the sons of the mayor (Joseph Calleia), the head of a rival family. Orso had no sympathy with what he considers the outmoded business of vendettas and bloody revenge, especially since he has fallen in love with an aristocratic English girl (Hillary Brooke) who is his guest, as is her titled father (Nigel Bruce). But Colomba, a passionate nationalist who objects to the French occupation of Corsica and who has an unduly strong love for her brother, stirs up the sentiments of her relatives and the community, and Orso is gradually drawn into conflict with the offending family. The bloody quest ends in the fog-shrouded hills with not only the death of the killers, but of Colomba, who gets in the way of a bullet and dies in her brother's arms.

When it was eventually finished in 1948, Hughes looked at the results and put *Vendetta* on the shelf. It was obviously a plodding picture. Perhaps it might build up a little interest by being talked about but not seen. That technique had worked splendidly with *The Outlaw.* With *Vendetta* there was not a whisper of interest. Hughes finally released it in November of 1950 as an RKO film, having sold it to the studio he now owned. The critics wasted no space in labeling it a costumed bore and placing the central blame on Faith Domergue, who, they said, was hopelessly out of her depth in a part that would have sunk even an experienced actress.

Hughes's instructions that Domergue was to be well photographed were met by fledgling director Ferrer, with the help of master cameraman Franz Planer, who captured her lovely visage in numerous close-ups. Composer Roy Webb also obeyed orders—the film was not scored until Hughes made it an RKO product—and provided a lush, tragic-romantic accompaniment that used an aria from Puccini's *Tosca.* Webb

The climax of *Vendetta* and the end of Colomba (Domergue), with George Dolenz.

was simply following orders, just as Victor Young had when he included themes by Tchaikowsky in his score for *The Outlaw*. But neither the photography nor the music could help *Vendetta*.

Although he would never admit it, Hughes must have had his own reservations about the film. He had designed it as a Faith Domergue showcase, but he shrewdly released *Where Danger Lives* a few months earlier than *Vendetta*. It co-starred her with Robert Mitchum and Claude Rains in a more commercial vehicle and one in which she was clearly more at ease. The critical consensus was that Domergue was a young lady of exotic beauty but not one who revealed any evidence of striking dramatic ability. That viewpoint would remain unchanged. Aside from loaning her out in 1946, along with Jane Russell, to appear in *Young Widow*, Hughes made only these two films with the girl with whom he was so impressed in 1940. Her contract expired in 1951 and he did not renew it. Domergue afterwards followed a spotty career in pictures over the next few years and eventually dropped out of the business. Like so many women who were involved with Hughes, she has always refrained from personal comment—except to shudder at the mention of *Vendetta*.

Howard Hughes, June 22, 1948, seated at his desk at the Samuel Goldwyn Studios, whence he ran the RKO Studios, two miles away.

RKO Hughes

The last film to bear the words, "Howard Hughes Presents."

In view of his long association with Hollywood, his enormous wealth, his obsessive-compulsive nature and a fascination with movies that lasted almost until the day he died, it was not surprising that Howard Hughes would one day own an entire motion picture studio. It was perhaps a little surprising that such a fiercely independent man, one who had always avoided the studio system, should want to involve himself in this kind of elaborate management, but his reasoning at the time no doubt convinced him that he could bring his own kind of management to bear and succeed. Hughes brought his own kind of management to RKO, but what he succeeded in doing was to bring the life of that studio to an end. No other chapter in Hollywood history compares in any way with Hughes's five years as the commandant of RKO.

At the time of his 1948 takeover the leading studios of Hollywood were—and still mostly are—MGM, Warners, Paramount, 20th Century-Fox, Universal, Columbia and RKO. Of them all RKO was the one with the most checkered history. It came into being with the advent of the sound era, when the Radio Corporation of America, which had acquired the FBO (Film Booking Offices of America) Studios, joined forces with the Keith-Albee-Orpheum theatre circuit. The merger was made in October of 1928, when it was decided to call the studio the Radio-Keith-Orpheum Corporation. It was a studio that turned out good, solid program product, occasionally highlighted by the Fred Astaire–Ginger Rogers musicals, the early Katharine Hepburn pictures and a few classics such as *Citizen Kane, Gunga Din,* and *The Hunchback of Notre Dame.*

By 1948 RKO had had more production managers and chains of

command than any other major studio. At this time the controlling owner and chairman of the board was Floyd Odlum, a financial tycoon who made no secret of not being interested in the esthetic value of films. All kinds of writings were on the Hollywood walls by late 1947, and Odlum began to look for a way out. The government's anti-trust laws were finally being levied, robbing the studios of their automatic film releasing systems through the theatre chains they owned; the town-industry was wracked with labor dissent; the anti-communist sentiment was casting an ugly pall over the picture business; and television was approaching like an oncoming juggernaut.

Odlum received a number of offers but he decided to deal with Hughes, which took months because he loved to dicker, ponder and negotiate. Hughes paid almost nine million dollars and became the principal stockholder in May of 1948. Hollywood was skeptical. RKO had not been doing well for a long time. Could it be that Hughes acquired it as a tax write-off? His business empire, especially the tool company and the aircraft company, were now worth hundreds of millions. Hughes denied this, saying he loved making movies, although a few of the harder-core skeptics suggested that buying a studio was at least a way of getting showings in the 124 RKO theatres for *The Sin of Harold Diddlebock*, now titled *Mad Wednesday*, and *Vendetta*, and possibly recouping the five million dollars he had spent making them. In the minds of ordinary businessmen this reasoning may have seemed absurd, but there was nothing ordinary about the mind of Howard Hughes, or his pride, or his doggedness, or his refusal to admit failure.

At the outset Hughes assured the two thousand employees of RKO that he was too busy with his other enterprises to involve himself in production, which came as a relief to them, since it was the thing they feared most. Hollywood legend has it that Hughes never once set foot inside his studio, but though it is true that all of his administration was done from his offices at the Goldwyn Studios, he did make one visit to RKO shortly after buying it. A witness to this visit was the esteemed director Fritz Lang, who had just made a western with Marlene Dietrich titled *Chuck-a-Luck*. Hughes told him to change the title to *Rancho Notorious* because Europeans would not be able to understand the other.

According to Lang, Hughes turned up one day with a large entourage and spent two hours walking around looking at every sound stage and construction shop, and said nothing to anyone except an exit instruction: "Paint it." Years later Hughes denied having said it, but it had soon become part of Hollywood lore.

The man who was most perturbed by the Hughes takeover was production head Dore Schary, an intellectual writer-producer whose concept of film making tended toward the idealistic. In 1938 he won an Oscar for his screenplay *Boys Town*, and in 1947 he had made *Crossfire* at RKO, one of Hollywood's first serious attacks on anti-Semitism. When he learned that Hughes might buy RKO he went to see Odlum to try and dissuade him, but idealistic arguments meant nothing to Odlum. After the purchase Schary handed in his resignation, feeling that he had nothing in common with Hughes. Hughes asked for a meeting at three o'clock one morning, but Schary refused to disturb a night's sleep since he was always at his desk by nine. Hughes, who was not used to people refusing a summons, set a more reasonable time. At the meeting Schary was asked to get rid of actress Barbara Bel Geddes because Hughes did not like her and to halt proposed production on the war film *Battleground*. Schary refused to do either. The meeting ended amicably, with an understanding that they were too dissimilar to work together.

Hughes accepted the resignation and asked Schary if he had any money due on his contract. Schary asked for nothing: "I told him, pointing out that he was tough and too rich for me to fight. He didn't smile. He stood up, ending the meeting, and I left. I felt unhappy that I was moving away from an unfinished job. Oddly enough, I also liked Hughes. Despite his strange behavior and rather curt manner, he was appealing and likable. A few weeks later I was asked to take over the production job at MGM. After the deal was set, I called Hughes and asked the price for *Battleground*. He wanted only what had been spent to write the script—about $20,000, plus some production drawings. It was a bargain. It was clear Hughes was a man who kept his word." Schary then proceeded to turn *Battleground* into a smash hit for MGM, but never openly boasted about his judgment. Hughes had believed that there was no market for war films at that time, and in a business as unpredictable as film, he could have been as right as he was wrong.

A year after Schary left he received a call from Hughes asking for another meeting. Schary was picked up and taken to the Hughes aircraft plant, only a few minutes from MGM in Culver City, where Hughes asked him to get into his small, nondescript Chevrolet. "We drove around the plant and, as he guided me, he spoke slowly but consistently, saying that he regretted that he had bought RKO, regretted that he had permitted me to leave, and that he was busy designing a new helicopter that could lift a freight car, and had so many interests that he found the operation of the studio an onerous one." However, Hughes had not called him to talk about aircraft production. He wanted some advice about the advertising campaign for the Roberto Rosselini picture *Stromboli*, which had become controversial because Rosselini had impregnated his married leading lady, Ingrid Bergman, and because Hughes's billboard and newspaper ads had been attacked by Hollywood as extremely distasteful. Did Schary agree? Schary said the ads were vulgar and not to Hughes's credit. Hughes thanked him and changed his campaign.

The impression that Hughes was a man who had little compassion for others is refuted by Dore Schary. When Schary became ill several years after taking over his job at MGM, and barely able to move, Hughes offered to fly him to any hospital in the country. Schary declined, but one day found Hughes calling upon him while he was recuperating at home. He wanted to know if there was anything he could do. Schary said there was not, and Hughes sat silently. Then he stood up and said, "If you want anything or need anything, let me know." Recalled Schary: "He turned and left the room. I was puzzled and also moved by his visit. I

105

had felt his loneliness and his inability to talk about it."

The compassion shown Dore Schary was in no way evident at RKO, which by the end of 1948 had become a panic-stricken studio. More than half the employees had either left or been laid off, production was down to a handful of projects, and losses were estimated to be in the millions. Fortunately the studio had a backlog of pictures to release and there was income from RKO's chain of theatres, plus income as the distributor of Disney and Goldwyn pictures. In terms of new productions all the worst fears of the producers were realized when Hughes questioned their every move and refused to allow anything to be released until he had viewed it and given approval, which often meant some re-editing, along with a painful period of time simply waiting for him to turn up. Hughes could only be reached by phone, if he could be reached at all, and almost everything was done through messengers. One producer summed up the misery of this method of production in one sentence: "Working for Hughes was like taking the ball in a football game and running four feet, only to find the coach was tackling you from behind."

The travails of RKO were not caused only by Howard Hughes. The other studios were also suffering losses due to declining theatre attendance. The great and wonderful boom enjoyed by Hollywood during the war years had ended. It was a new world, never to be the same. American public tastes and habits were altering and the international film market was also not what it used to be. In March of 1949 the RKO stockholders agreed to split their theatre organization from the production company. The great crunch had finally arrived, and the other studios were forced to follow suit. It was the most momentus decision ever faced by Hollywood and it spelled an end to the Golden Days. The studio system was on the way out.

One of the first films Hughes put into production was titled *It's Only Money*, in which he starred Jane Russell with Frank Sinatra and Groucho Marx. The title became a bad joke on the RKO lot because of the production delays caused by Hughes, all of which wasted needed funds. Russell was still under personal contract to Hughes and he loaned her to RKO for a string of films. The film was not released until 1951, almost three years after it was started, at which time the title became *Double Dynamite*, with Russell's presence obviously alluded to in the advertising as "double delicious, double delightful and double delirious." The critics claimed it was barely single entertaining. Its production woes were sadly caused by the judgment of a man who was much too busy with other businesses, especially with the outbreak of the Korean War and his aircraft company's involvement in producing war machines.

Executives and producers came and went in these years like comedians in an unfunny farce, as RKO struggled to stay afloat. The struggles became even more painful as Hollywood was enmeshed in the anti-communist crusade, of which Hughes was a leading light. Politically to the extreme right, he flailed against any possible left-wing sympathies in any production in which he had a hand, and any member of a cast or crew who may have differed in that regard was wise to keep his own counsel. Hughes was not alone in this stance—most of Hollywood's upper echelon moguls felt the same way.

A ray of hope shined across RKO in the summer of 1950 when Hughes brought the team of Jerry Wald and Norman Krasna to the studio. He had bought up the contract of this brilliant pair of producers from Warners and gave them an understanding that they could plan production on sixty films with a fifty-million-dollar budget. It was a time of elation, and Wald crowed about their autonomy and artistic control, as Krasna outlined a program of quality products. The first of the RKO-Wald-Krasna pictures was a mild comedy, *Behave Yourself,* with Farley Granger and Shelley Winters, but it was followed by three excellent films: *The Blue Veil,* with Jane Wyman as a dedicated governess; *Clash by Night,* with Fritz Lang directing Barbara Stanwyck and Robert Ryan in a love tragedy; and *The Lusty Men,* starring Robert Mitchum in one of the best films ever made about rodeo cowboys. On the face of it, it was an impressive listing, but those involved in the films witnessed that Wald and Krasna were constantly questioned by Hughes. After those four films the team asked for, and received, their release from RKO.

In September of 1952 Hughes, having weathered endless production conflicts and the sometimes vicious battles he waged against communism in Hollywood, decided he had had enough. He owned twenty-five percent of the stock of RKO and he now put his shares on the market. They were bought by a Chicago syndicate of financiers, headed by Ralph Stolkin. The price was settled at $7.35 million, with a down payment of $1.25 million, which allowed the group to take control of RKO in October. Within weeks of these negotiations *The Wall Street Journal* ran a series of articles which exposed the dubious backgrounds of most of the men in the syndicate, including Stolkin, who had been engaged in illicit mail order operations. Some of the others were connected with organized crime. Hollywood, still reeling under the humiliation dealt it by the findings of the House Un-American Activities Committee, was horrified and petrified.

The reaction of the film community and the undeniable evidence presented by *The Wall Street Journal* resulted in the members of the syndicate surrendering their claims on RKO. With no buyers for their offered shares, they returned the stock to Hughes, which cost them their down payment. A little richer, Hughes began 1953 once again as the commanding officer of RKO but faced with a barrage of lawsuits from other stockholders, who claimed, with some justification, that the studio had been badly run and that it had lost tens of millions since he took it over. Instead of making movies Hughes now found himself involved in endless legal battles, requiring batteries of lawyers. Actor Dick Powell, then at the studio to make his debut as a director with *Split Second,* quipped, "RKO's contract list is now down to three actors and 127 lawyers." Hughes's adventures in the movie business had turned into a nightmare. A solution had to be found, and it was—but it was such a drastic and surprising one that it took the wind out of the sails of friend and foe alike.

107

On February 8, 1954, Hughes astonished the financial establishment by announcing that he was willing to purchase every existing RKO share at six dollars, which was twice the market value. To do this Hughes would have to come up with $23,489,478 in cash. He issued this statement: "There have been expressions of dissatisfaction among stockholders. I have been sued by certain of the stockholders and accused of responsibility for losses of the corporation. I would like to feel that I have given all the shareholders of RKO Pictures Corporation an opportunity to receive for their stock an amount well in excess of the market value at the time when I first became connected with the company." Along with the announcement came a notice that the board of directors would have to accept the offer in a week and that the deadline for the transfer of stock would expire two months later.

Since the total of all the stockholders' suits against him was in the region of thirty million dollars, and since Hughes's complete ownership of RKO would give him assets and property worth a possible hundred million, it was not such an outlandish offer. It was outlandish only in the sense that no one in Hollywood had ever before made a cash offer of such proportions, and no one man had ever completely owned a major film studio.

Had Hughes been able to totally acquire RKO he would have merged it with Hughes Tool Company, thereby allowing him to offset the RKO losses and legal costs against a wealthy parent. But the master plan was spoiled by the machinations of an old business acquaintance who had now set himself up as the enemy—Floyd Odlum—who was offended because Hughes had not kept his promise to let him have first crack at the purchase of the RKO theatre chain after the chain had been divorced from the production company. Hughes instead sold it to New England industrialist Albert A. List. Before the stockholders could come to their appointed time of decision, Odlum had bought up all the stock he could get, until he had almost as much as Hughes. He and Odlum dickered and haggled for month after wearying month. United Press correspondent Aline Mosby commented, "The most exciting plot in Hollywood today is behind the camera—a real-life fight between two financial wizards for control of RKO."

At one point during these long months of infighting and legal manipulations, Hughes was heard to say, "I need RKO like I need the plague." In July of 1955 he decided he had had enough of the seemingly impossible dealings with Odlum and sold RKO to General Teleradio, Inc., a subsidiary of General Tire and Rubber, a huge corporation based in Akron, Ohio. The president of General Teleradio, Thomas F. O'Neil, flew to Los Angeles to negotiate with Hughes and found, as had many others, that it was a protracted process. Hughes was then living at the Beverly Hills Hotel, where O'Neil spent three days and nights presenting and countering deals. O'Neil was exhausted by it all, as well as being amazed by Hughes's business savvy. He told a reporter, "That man didn't need a lawyer. He knows more about corporate law than any attorney I ever met."

Hughes sold RKO for $25,000,000, almost a quarter of which was his after the stockholders were paid off, not to mention a huge pile of legal costs. He had also earned profit on the sale of the theatre chain, plus keeping the forfeited deposit of the Chicago syndicate. All in all it is estimated that Hughes cleared some six million dollars on the sale to General Teleradio. He seemed to show more relief than delight. It had been a gruelling five years and it had not brought him any real satisfaction. On the other hand, he could hardly have picked a worse time in Hollywood history to choose to run a film studio.

Much has been made of Hughes's mismanagement of RKO, but it is doubtful if the studio could have prospered under any commander in these difficult years when television was changing the basis of American entertainment. Movie theatres were closing by the hundreds, and eventually the only way the major studios could survive was to get into the business of producing TV product. When O'Neil took over he assured Hollywood that his company would remain in the motion picture business, but it was obvious that General Teleradio's main interest in buying RKO was in acquiring its library of almost a thousand films, which soon became a source of endless television income. The life of RKO as a feature film production company came to an end in the fall of 1957 when O'Neil sold the studio to Desilu, the television company owned by Lucille Ball and Desi Arnaz.

The reign of Howard Hughes as the boss of RKO may have been chaotic but it was not, as is sometimes supposed, non-productive. Much was produced in those five years, and while it can be argued that few of the pictures were very profitable, the same can be said of much of the product turned out by MGM, Warners, Paramount, 20th Century-Fox, *et al.*

The following are the RKO films made under the supervision of Howard Hughes:

Bill Williams, Grandon Rhodes and Barbara Hale in *The Clay Pigeon.*

109

THE CLAY PIGEON (1949)

The first film made at RKO after Hughes took over was a modest but taut programmer running 63 minutes, directed by Richard Fleischer and written by Carl Foreman, two fine film makers in the early stages of their careers. The leading character is a sailor (Bill Williams) who awakens in a hospital and finds himself charged with treason because he brought about the death of a friend in a Japanese prison camp by informing on him. Having been in a coma, he cannot remember anything, so he kidnaps the widow (Barbara Hale) in order to learn about the charges. She believes him and joins him in helping to reveal the culprit, the actual informer who is now engaged in counterfeiting. Fleischer's direction made *The Clay Pigeon* a tense and suspenseful picture.

THE BIG STEAL (1949)

Robert Mitchum spent ten years at RKO, including the whole period with Hughes in command. He was the studio's leading male player and he made more pictures with Hughes than any other actor. At the time of the Hughes takeover, Mitchum was under arrest because of his use of marijuana. Hughes used his influence with the law, claiming that a large cast and crew were idle because Mitchum was being detained. The actor was released on bail and *The Big Steal* was mostly filmed while he awaited sentencing. During the two months Mitchum was in jail, director Don Siegel used a double and filmed all the long-shot action sequences, such as the car chases, and when Mitchum returned they filled in the remaining scenes. RKO's concern that Mitchum's run-in with the law might harm him at the box office proved groundless, and the public flocked to see *The Big Steal*, which was actually a big chase as Army officer Mitchum pursued the villains who had made off with a $300,000 Army payroll and crossed the border into Mexico (where much of the film was shot).

Hughes could have dropped Mitchum by citing the morality clause that was standard in all actors' contracts, but he did not. He accurately guessed that Mitchum's mild notoriety would aid his popularity, and he also admired him. Mitchum's cool, flippant nonconformity was to Hughes's taste, and he advanced the actor $50,000 to cover his legal fees—to be deducted from future earnings.

FOLLOW ME QUIETLY (1949)

Richard Fleischer was the director of this 60-minute B picture, starring William Lundigan as a police inspector assigned to apprehend a maniacal killer who has been terrorizing a city. A girl crime reporter

William Bendix, John Qualen, Jane Greer, Patric Knowles and Robert Mitchum in *The Big Steal.*

(Dorothy Patrick) bothers the inspector with the questioning necessary to get a story on his career, but proves valuable in helping him track his quarry, a mild-mannered wierdo who commits his crimes only on rainy nights. *Follow Me Quietly* was designed as the bottom half of a double bill and doubtless served its purpose.

William Lundigan and Dorothy Patrick in *Follow Me Quietly.*

111

STRANGE BARGAIN (1949)

A bargain of a B picture. Jeffrey Lynn and Martha Scott are a married couple having trouble making ends meet; he is laid off when the investment firm for whom he has been working goes bankrupt, but one of the employers promises to take care of him if Lynn will partake of an insurance fraud. The scheme involves the employer (Richard Gaines) faking his suicide, a plan that goes awry when the employer is found to be really dead and Lynn the prime suspect. The villain is the employer's widow (Katherine Emory), who also plans to kill Lynn because he knows too much. He is, of course, saved in the nick of time. Director Will Price drew praise for his pacing and construction of this neat little mystery drama.

A DANGEROUS PROFESSION (1949)

Two actors who came to stardom in Hughes production—Pat (*The Front Page*) O'Brien and George (*Scarface*) Raft—found themselves working for their old boss, although in a conventional crime movie that would come and go without much notice. In this they are partners in a bail bond company; when one of their clients, a suspected robber (Bill Williams) is mysteriously killed they set out to unravel the mystery, partly because Raft is smitten with the dead man's lovely widow (Ella Raines). Director Ted Tetzlaff brought the picture in at a fast clip, which he surely realized was the only way to deal with this kind of slick programmer.

THE THREAT (1949)

The old yarn about the convict who escapes prison and vows to wipe out the cop who put him there received a first-rate treatment in this outing, perhaps because the man who wrote it, Hugh King, also produced it. The film's chief asset is Charles McGraw as the tough, steely crook, who captures Los Angeles private eye Michael O'Shea, singer Virginia Grey and district attorney Frank Conroy, all of whom he believes had a hand in putting him away and must therefore pay with their lives. They almost do in the 66 minutes of this well made and directed (by Felix Feist) movie that was designed as the bottom half of a double bill but which probably provided more entertainment than the picture with which it was playing.

Jeffrey Lynn and Martha Scott in *Strange Bargain*.

Pat O'Brien and George Raft in *A Dangerous Profession*.

Michael O'Shea and Virginia Grey in *The Threat*.

113

HOLIDAY AFFAIR (1949)

With *The Big Steal* a hit and Robert Mitchum's popularity increased rather than decreased by his stint in jail, Howard Hughes decided to put him in RKO's 1949 Christmas offering, giving him an uncharacteristic role as a department store toy salesman, opposite Janet Leigh as a comparison shopper. Hughes had borrowed Leigh from MGM's Dore Schary for a couple of pictures, the second of which, *Jet Pilot*, would not emerge until 1957. In this charming but not very convincing Isobel Lennart screenplay, Leigh cannot afford to buy her son (Gordon Gebert) the electric train he wants, and Mitchum wins both their hearts by playing Santa Claus. *Holiday Affair* did not bring much Christmas cheer to RKO and director-producer Don Hartman afterwards left the studio, claiming that working under Hughes was too restrictive for his temperament.

ARMORED CAR ROBBERY (1950)

As a reward for his fine performance in *The Threat*, Hughes gave Charles McGraw top billing and put him on the right side of the law in this neatly made crime yarn about a master criminal (William Talman) who seizes a fortune-laden armored car. Two of his henchmen are killed in the attempt but the crook and his stripteaser girl friend (Adele Jergens) almost get away with the heist, with the bulldog detective making the difference. The chase ends at Los Angeles International Airport, with the fleeing crook being bowled over by an incoming airplane. Richard Fleischer added to his growing laurels as a director, and McGraw's acting assured him plenty of further work.

THE WHITE TOWER (1950)

For this, one of RKO's bigger budget projects (shot in Technicolor), cast and crew were transported to Switzerland for a tale about the courageous and fanatically determined people who climb mountains. Hughes borrowed Italian actress Alida Valli from David O. Selznick and cast her as a girl who wants to climb the White Tower because her father died in the attempt. Her party is made up of an English scientist (Sir Cedric Hardwicke), an alcoholic French novelist (Claude Rains), an ex-Nazi officer (Lloyd Bridges), a Swiss guide (Oscar Homolka) and a young American ex-bomber pilot (Glenn Ford), more interested in the girl than in scaling precipices. The handsome film is basically a study of its six characters, with the trek revealing their humanity or lack thereof. Two die in the scaling and none of the others reach the top. The girl finally realizes that love is a greater attainment than climbing a mountain. Ted Tetzlaff directed, but much of the film's success was due to master color photographer Ray Rennahan.

Robert Mitchum and Janet Leigh in
Holiday Affair.

William Talman, Don McGuire and Adele
Jergens in *Armored Car Robbery.*

Oscar Homolka, Glenn Ford, Alida Valli
and Lloyd Bridges in *The White Tower.*

115

WHERE DANGER LIVES (1950)

This far in his regime Howard Hughes had supervised his RKO films without too much involvement in their production. But there were a few films in which he took close interest, and this was one of them. He had a strong liking for Robert Mitchum, who referred to his boss as "The Phantom," since no one at RKO ever saw him, except for those few who had meetings with him in other places. Hughes was particularly concerned about *Where Danger Lives* because it was vehicle for Faith Domergue, and it can truly be said that he needed to justify his faith in her. To create more interest in the limp *Vendetta*, he wanted her to be seen first in something more arresting. In this she is a beautiful psychopath who lures a doctor (Mitchum) and involves him in the murder of her rich, elderly husband (Claude Rains). The doctor thinks he is responsible for the death, but the wife is the real culprit. She ends up being shot while trying to cross into Mexico, but clears the name of the doctor before expiring. Hughes brought in the veteran John Farrow to direct this murky, implausible tale, but even his skill could not reveal any genuine acting ability on the part of the leading lady. Hughes gave up Faith.

BUNCO SQUAD (1950)

With such a title and a running time of 67 minutes the public could get only what was obvious—a B picture; but as with most of RKO's entries in their field it was a good, solid little movie. It starred Robert Sterling as a police inspector detailed to investigate the doings of a group of phony psychics and seers led by suave Ricardo Cortez. Director Herbert I. Leeds whipped the material along in the semi-documentary, crime-exposé style that had taken hold in Hollywood by 1950.

BORN TO BE BAD (1950)

Barbara Bel Geddes was scheduled to star in this treatment of the novel *All Kneeling* by Anne Parrish, with Dore Schary producing it under the title *Bed of Roses*. One of the first things Hughes did at RKO was to dump Bel Geddes, change the title and bring in Joan Fontaine. With the excellent Nicholas Ray as director the end results produced a hit for the studio and another one of Fontaine's portraits of beautiful ladies who look innocent and kind but who actually have souls like cobras. Here she is an operator in San Francisco society who steals millionaire Zachary Scott away from Joan Leslie and marries him, but soon starts an affair with novelist Robert Ryan. Eventually she is rejected by both of them. Today this kind of material is the stuff of TV soap operas; in 1950 it was made acceptable by the finesse of Fontaine, the fine talent of Ryan and the sort of production values—sets, costumes, music scoring, photography—that had become standard in all the major studios.

116

Faith Domergue and Robert Mitchum in *Where Danger Lives.*

Joan Dixon and Robert Sterling in *Bunco Squad.*

Joan Fontaine and Robert Ryan in *Born to Be Bad.*

NEVER A DULL MOMENT (1950)

A film with a title like *Never a Dull Moment* needs to be brilliant to avoid the sarcasm of critics. This one was not, although most viewers conceded it had some good moments, thanks to the skill of such light-comedy players as Irene Dunne and Fred MacMurray. Here she is a New York song writer and he is a rancher appearing in a rodeo in order to make some badly needed money. They fall in love and marry, and the sophisticated New Yorker goes through the pains of adjusting to life in the west, which includes suffering the pranks of his daughters Gigi Perreau and Natalie Wood, who soon decide Irene is a good sport. She returns to New York to write with her former partner because her rancher husband is again in need of funds, but finds Manhattan impossible. She gladly goes back to the ranch. Another old hand at this kind of thing, director George Marshall, helped pull it all together.

HUNT THE MAN DOWN (1951)

Gig Young headed the cast of this 68-minute whodunit as a Los Angeles public defender assigned to defend a man (James Anderson) who had evaded the law for twelve years and who maintains that he is innocent of the murder charge laid against him. Plodding and persistent work on the part of the defender eventually brings to justice the real killer. George Archainbaud's brisk direction made the film less tedious than it might otherwise have been.

THE COMPANY SHE KEEPS (1951)

John Houseman, many years before he turned to acting, was the producer and John Cromwell, with a solid twenty-year track record, was the director, but even their talents failed to make *The Company She Keeps* any more than passing product. It is the story of a woman parole officer (Lizabeth Scott), an ex-convict (Jane Greer) and a newspaperman (Dennis O'Keefe). He is the boyfriend of the parole officer, until he falls in love with the glamorous parolee and wants to marry her. The good-hearted parole officer feels she cannot stand in the way, even though she knows the parolee is not worth the man she must give up. He, of course, finally sees the light. Unfortunately, neither Houseman nor Cromwell could see the light before they started on this limp yarn.

Irene Dunne, Fred MacMurray and Andy Devine in *Never a Dull Moment*.

Harry Shannon, Gig Young and Iris Adrian in *Hunt the Man Down*.

Jane Greer and Dennis O'Keefe in *The Company She Keeps*.

119

GAMBLING HOUSE (1951)

Terry Moore claims she was once married to Howard Hughes, but for all the time she may have spent with him she appeared in only one of his films. For this picture he had to borrow her from Columbia, to co-star her with Victor Mature, whom he borrowed from 20th Century-Fox. The results of all the dickering involved hardly justified the end result, a pedestrian movie about a social worker (Moore) who civilizes a rough, Italian-born gambler (Mature) who has never taken out citizenship. By the time she has done with him he has beaten a deportation charge, caused a big-time hood (William Bendix) to be shot by his own men, contributed some of that hood's money to needy welfare cases and become a citizen. Love has seldom conquered so much. RKO workhorse director Ted Tetzlaff did his best to make this material as plausible as he could.

MY FORBIDDEN PAST (1951)

Ann Sheridan was slated to star in *My Forbidden Past*, the screen version of Polan Banks's best-selling 1947 novel *Carriage Entrance*, but the production was delayed so long by Hughes that she sued him for $350,000, claiming the delay was injurious to her career. An out-of-court settlement was arrived at, with a guarantee that Sheridan would be used in a later RKO production, which turned out to be the 1953 *Appointment in Honduras*. Hughes replaced her with Ava Gardner, with whom he was then socially involved, and gave her Robert Mitchum as her co-star. The teaming was good but the stars could not bring the preposterous story to life. It featured Gardner as a late-nineteenth-century New Orleans lady of society, whose grandmother was the kind who did anything and everything to gain wealth. When she becomes heir to that fortune she goes after medical professor Mitchum, even though he is married. When his wife is accidentally killed, Mitchum is accused of murder, but Gardner brings information to the inquest that clears him. In doing so she has to reveal her family's dark secrets, none of which keep her out of the arms of Mitchum. Robert Stevenson directed with a firm hand, but he was not able to bring much excitement to this opulent but musty picture.

BEST OF THE BADMEN (1951)

A whole decade after he was hired by Hughes for *The Outlaw*, Jack Buetel finally appeared in another film, still as an outlaw. In this post-Civil War western he is one of the ex-Confederate guerillas who team up with ex-Union Army officer Robert Ryan to wage war on Robert Preston and his illicit empire. It may have been a dubious accounting of history, but *Best of the Badmen*, with Technicolor, masses of horses and gunfire, and brisk direction by William D. Russell, pleased the many western fans thoughout the world, which is precisely what it was designed to do.

Terry Moore and Victor Mature in *Gambling House.*

Ava Gardner, Melvyn Douglas and Robert Mitchum in *My Forbidden Past.*

Jack Buetel, Walter Brennan, Claire Trevor and Robert Ryan in *Best of the Badmen.*

121

ROADBLOCK (1951)

Charles McGraw was promoted from the B picture division and given the lead in this minor but interestingly different crime picture. Director Harold Daniels's emphasis is on action in this story of a top-notch insurance company investigator (McGraw) who goes astray because of his love for a beautiful playgirl (Joan Dixon). He engineers a large heist to get the money to marry the girl, only to find that she genuinely loves him, money or not. Not knowing what else to do, they try to make their way out of Los Angeles, but a former fellow investigator (Louis Jean Heydt) has solved the theft and tracked down McGraw, causing the police to seal every exit. In trying to escape by driving along the Los Angeles river, with its concrete causeway and shoulders, McGraw is trapped and killed. McGraw's performance as the decent man gone wrong and the director's realistic handling of the material make *Roadblock* an interesting item in the collection of crime movies.

FLYING LEATHERNECKS (1951)

John Wayne liked Howard Hughes and vice versa. They each admired individuality and independence, and their political views were in accord. Wayne accepted Hughes's offer to come to RKO and appear in any kind of film he chose to make. *Jet Pilot* was first, but with the picture constantly held back because of ever-changing aerial footage being brought in by Hughes, Wayne agreed to make yet another movie about aviation in the South Pacific in the Second World War. In this he is a tough, rock-ribbed disciplinarian major, heading up a fighter squadron and earning the dislike of his second in command (Robert Ryan) and most of his pilots, until they realize that this is what it takes to win a war. Tight direction by Nicholas Ray and excellent aerial sequences made *Flying Leathernecks* a superior picture of its kind. It was on this film that Hughes took his first RKO credit, "Howard Hughes Presents."

HIS KIND OF WOMAN (1951)

Hughes had Jane Russell under personal contract, so it was obvious he would use her at RKO. Pairing her with the studio's top male attraction was equally obvious, and successful. In this mystery adventure set in Mexico, Robert Mitchum is a gambler who gets involved with a deported American mobster (Raymond Burr) and Russell is a sultry nightclub singer who falls for him and dumps her actor boyfriend (Vincent Price). The gambler's life is on the line because the mobster wants to have a plastic surgeon arrange his face to resemble that of the gambler and eliminate the original. John Farrow directed all the complicated plot lines and the chases with appropriate skill, although at 122 minutes the film was far longer than the 1951 average. In pairing Mitchum and Russell, Hughes got all the mileage out of the teaming that was possible.

Joan Dixon and Charles McGraw in
Roadblock.

J.C. Flippen. Robert Ryan and John Wayne
in *Flying Leathernecks*.

Vincent Price, Tim Holt, Jane Russell and
Robert Mitchum in *His Kind of Woman*.

123

The costume designers were instructed to pay particular attention to the Russell figure, which together with her good singing voice made *His Kind of Woman* her best showcase to date. However, because of this being her first RKO picture, Hughes pondered over the editing and release. And due to his involvement in other things, months drifted by as the RKO production office waited for him to view the film (this also applied to many others), and as a consequence *His Kind of Woman* reached the screen in July of 1951, a year after it had been completed.

THE WHIP HAND (1951)

At the beginning of its filming, *The Whip Hand* was about Hitler being found alive in America and plotting his revenge, but after viewing the early material Hughes decided against the Hitler angle and had the dramatic emphasis put on the communists. Here a magazine writer (Elliott Reid) stumbles on a remote community in Wisconsin while on his vacation and learns that they are plotting the overthrow of America by means of chemical warfare. His snooping leads to his capture, but the FBI turns up in the nick of time. *The Whip Hand*, one of the few films directed by Hollywood's master production designer William Cameron Menzies, was a little too intense in its anti-communism to bring in any profits. The lead actress, Carla Balenda, was under personal contract to Hughes, but after this weak outing the odds around RKO were that she would not last for long.

THE RACKET (1951)

The only one of his films Hughes ever remade was *The Racket*, updating the silent 1928 picture to one which tied in with the attacks by Senator Estes Kefauver and his Senate Crime Investigating Committee, which were headline news in the early 1950's. Robert Mitchum and Robert Ryan were given the roles originally played by Thomas Meighan and Louis Wolheim, those of the incorruptible policeman and the vicious racketeer who had been childhood chums. W. R. Burnett and William Wister Haines updated the old Bartlett Cromack play, and John Cromwell, who had been an actor in the original company of that play, was the director. This version of *The Racket* fared well at the box office, but it was the superb performance of Ryan as the fanatic, repulsive villain that drew all the critical comment.

TWO TICKETS TO BROADWAY (1951)

This musical is the source of one of the most frequently recalled stories about Howard Hughes. He kept his offices at the Goldwyn studios and not at RKO, but since he wanted to see the sets for the finale of *Two*

Otto Waldis, Elliott Reid and Raymond
Burr in *The Whip Hand.*

Robert Ryan and William Talman in *The
Racket.*

Tony Martin and Janet Leigh in *Two
Tickets to Broadway.*

125

Tickets to Broadway, he ordered them dismantled and erected on a Goldwyn sound stage so that he might view them. After he saw and approved the sets, they were then hauled back to RKO and reassembled. The effort and expense were hardly justified, because the picture turned out to be mild, despite having the fabled Busby Berkeley as its dance director. He was not given much to work with in this yarn about a girl (Janet Leigh) from Vermont who goes to New York to make a name for herself on Broadway. After the usual trials and tribulations made familiar by this kind of movie musical, she gets work on the Bob Crosby TV Show. Tony Martin, Gloria DeHaven and Ann Miller contributed to the seven musical numbers, none of which made a lasting impression. Director James V. Kern managed to bring it all together at 106 minutes.

DOUBLE DYNAMITE (1951)

The only place in film history in which *Double Dynamite* is likely to be found is in the game of Trivial Pursuit. In which film did Frank Sinatra and Groucho Marx sing a duet? The name of the song is also the original title of this picture, *It's Only Money,* which was completed in late 1949 but not released until November of 1951. The long delay was caused by the obviously disappointing results of teaming Sinatra and Marx with Jane Russell in a poor script, although Hughes tried to whip up interim interest with publicity, again stressing the physical endowments of Russell and the leering persona of Groucho. Sinatra had started in first place but it was a time of diminishing popularity for him, and, since Hughes disliked him anyway, Sinatra ended up with third billing. Director Irving Cummings tried to inject some life into this limp vehicle but, except for Groucho's flippant cracks, failed. It is a yarn about a mild bank clerk (Sinatra) who cannot persuade his girlfriend (Russell) that he has won $60,000 at the racetrack on the day that a similar amount has been stolen from his bank. Groucho is the waiter in the restaurant where the lovers meet for lunch every day—and his presence is the only reason to see the film.

ON DANGEROUS GROUND (1952)

If there is one consistently strong line running through the Hughes RKO years it is the acting of the remarkable Robert Ryan, a man whose skill as a film actor has never been fully recognized. In this dark melodrama he is a police detective whose days spent dealing with human dregs have turned him into a tough, sour man. His character undergoes a change when he is assigned to a murder case in the country, where a young girl has been slaughtered. He sees that the father (Ward Bond) is the same kind of brutal, unthinking man as he himself is, and he learns compassion from the blind sister (Ida Lupino) of the killer, a mentally deficient young man (Sumner Williams). The film was not a winner at the box office but it was an honorable entry, with fine direction by Nicholas Ray and a superb musical score by Bernard Herrmann.

Groucho Marx and Frank Sinatra in
Double Dynamite.

Ward Bond and Robert Ryan in *On
Dangerous Ground.*

127

A GIRL IN EVERY PORT (1952)

Groucho Marx had little luck in the movies after breaking up with his brothers. *A Girl in Every Port* did little to lead him to believe he could make it on his own. In this mostly feeble comedy he is paired with William Bendix as a pair of sailors who somehow acquire a pair of twin race horses, selling one and racing the other until both cause a problem by coming in as a tie in the same race. Their strained relationship with the Navy ends when they capture some saboteurs. Director Chester Erskine could blame no one other than himself for this limp stuff, because he wrote the screenplay himself. Groucho retired from the movies, with this one, except for a cameo in the even more dreadful *The Story of Mankind*, a 1957 Warner Bros. bomb.

THE LAS VEGAS STORY (1952)

The drama behind the making of this film was more trenchant than anything on screen. When Howard Hughes learned that writer Paul Jarrico had once belonged to the Communist Party, he refused to allow his name in the credits, resulting in Jarrico's suing Hughes and bringing the weight of the Writers Guild of America to bear. Some critics pointed out that Jarrico was lucky not to have this name on the picture, which concerned itself with a nightclub singer (Jane Russell) who marries a man (Vincent Price) on the rebound from the slick gambler (Victor Mature) she really loves. Life for all of them becomes chaotic when each is involved in the same robbery and murder in wicked Las Vegas. Robert Stevenson directed this dismal tale, whose only charm is the presence of Hoagy Carmichael singing a couple of his fine songs.

AT SWORD'S POINT (1952)

Hollywood squeezed a little more juice out of Alexander Dumas's *The Three Musketeers* by inventing children for D'Artagnan and his lusty comrades, who follow in parental footsteps and defend the French throne against usurpers. Cornel Wilde, one of the few celluloid swash-bucklers who had actually been a fencing champion, was D'Artagnan junior and the offspring of Athos turned out to be gorgeous Maureen O'Hara, who could use a rapier equally as well as the boys. The picture contained nothing that had not been seen before, but the Technicolor, excellent swordplay and Lewis Allen's spirited direction made it an enjoyable romp of its kind.

William Bendix and Groucho Marx in *A Girl in Every Port.*

Jane Russell and Hoagy Carmichael in *The Las Vegas Story.*

Maureen O'Hara, Cornel Wilde, Gladys Cooper, Dan O'Herlihy and Alan Hale, Jr., in *At Sword's Point.*

129

THE PACE THAT THRILLS (1952)

Sixty-three minutes in the world of motorcycle racing, whipped along at a fast clip by director Leon Barsha and co-starring Bill Williams as a cocky racer employed by a bike manufacturer (Robert Armstrong) and Carla Balenda as a newspaper reporter who considers the racer an unfair rogue and blasts away at him in her column. The rogue falls in love with the reporter and starts to see the error of his ways. In the end he deliberately loses a race so that a rival can win, but in losing he wins the heart of the reporter. But only a lover of motorcycle racing could love this film.

MACAO (1952)

The success of *His Kind of Woman* made a reteaming of Robert Mitchum and Jane Russell a certainty. Josef von Sternberg, who had signed a contract with Hughes to direct two pictures, found himself given this assignment after doing *Jet Pilot*, which would not be seen for years. Von Sternberg was bitter about both pictures, claiming in his autobiography that half a dozen Hughes aids constantly interfered all through the production. *Macao*, made entirely at the RKO studios with Far East backshots, presents Mitchum as an adventurer who has left the States to avoid arrest for a crime he did not commit, and Russell as (again) a nightclub singer with a cynical regard for men. Detective William Bendix uses them as pawns in his attempt to track down jewel smugglers operating out of this Portuguese island off the Chinese coast. Despite the claimed interference, Von Sternberg managed to give *Macao* some of the dark, exotic style for which he was famous, and for an itinerant singer Russell was conspicuously well attired, most noticeably in one gold and silver lamé gown that looked as if it had been sprayed on her.

THE HALF-BREED (1952)

Hughes still had Jack Buetel under contract and still refused to be swayed by the general opinion that Buetel would never be an actor. By this time Hollywood had arrived at the probability that not all American Indians were villains, and *The Half-Breed* attempts to adjust the balance with a tale about a part Apache (Buetel) who tries to bring peace between his two blood lines and finds opposition in a politican (Reed Hadley) whose chief interest lies in filching gold from Apache lands. He does, however, find an ally in a gambler (Robert Young), who helps him end the career of the dreadful politician. Director Stuart Gilmore clearly had trouble breathing life into this account, partly because of the implausible casting of the leading man.

Frank McHugh and Bill Williams in *The Pace That Thrills*.

Jane Russell in *Macao*.

Janis Carter and Jack Buetel in *The Half-Breed*.

THE NARROW MARGIN (1952)

With *The Narrow Margin* RKO proved what it had proven many times before—that its modestly budgeted B pictures (this one cost a quarter of a million dollars) were often better entertainment than its more pretentious investments. Here the reliable Charles McGraw, aided by equally reliable director Richard Fleischer, is a tough Chicago policeman assigned to guard a gangster's widow on the train ride to Los Angeles, where she is to testify before a grand jury. Since the opposition does not know what she looks like, they eliminate a number of suspects en route, and the woman McGraw thinks is the widow is actually a policewoman (Marie Windsor), sent to test his loyalty. Fast pacing, suspense and fine acting from the two leads makes this an almost textbook example in the once flourishing art of making B pictures.

ONE MINUTE TO ZERO (1952)

Charles McGraw was given leads in B pictures, but in the A category he was relegated to supporting player. In this story of the Korean War he is a U.S. Army sergeant under the command of Brigadier General Robert Mitchum, a tough, front-line soldier whose battlefield attentions are somewhat deflected by a sincere United Nations representative (Ann Blyth) who does not quite understand what war is all about. She not only finds out, but she wins the love of the young general. Tay Garnett, a director usually at home with action pictures, was unable to do much with this conventional material, other than to spike it with some genuine Korean War footage, which tended to make the studio sequences even more unrealistic.

MONTANA BELLE (1952)

A mere listing of Jane Russell's films is no indication of the order in which they were made. In 1948, after she had made only *The Outlaw* and *Young Widow*, Hughes loaned her to producer Howard Welsch to play bandit queen Belle Starr in the western *Montana Belle*. After looking at it, Hughes decided to buy it and release it through RKO. He also decided, wisely, to hang onto it until Russell had appeared in several more succcessful pictures. *Montana Belle* did not emerge until late 1952, at which time it did nothing to advance her career because it was a weak picture, and one in which she looked ungainly. In this silly yarn she falls in love with a bandit (Scott Brady) and joins his gang, but falls victim to all the double-crossing between the members. The man who really lovers her is a gambler (George Brent), who promises to be waiting for her when she gets out of jail. Allan Dwan, a director since 1914, steered this nonsense as best he could.

132

Marie Windsor and Charles McGraw in *The Narrow Margin.*

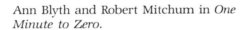

Ann Blyth and Robert Mitchum in *One Minute to Zero.*

Jack Lambert, Jane Russell, Scott Brady and Forrest Tucker in *Montana Belle.*

133

BLACKBEARD THE PIRATE (1952)

Robert Newton was a fine actor, except when drunk, when his work became florid and hammy. Watching him as *Blackbeard the Pirate*, it is reasonable to assume that he was drunk all through the shooting. With the great Raoul Walsh as director—the same man who had drawn fine swashbuckling performances out of the equally difficult Errol Flynn— the viewer can also assume that Walsh did not care much. Newton rumbles around the screen bellowing talk about murder, pillage and larceny, when not squabbling with Sir Henry Morgan (Torin Thatcher). Linda Darnell, who was socializing with Howard Hughes at the time, wanders around the picture carrying on an affair with a doctor-pirate (Keith Andes), but she could have been forgiven if she had wandered toward the exit.

ANGEL FACE (1953)

Jean Simmons came to Hollywood in 1950 when her husband Stewart Granger was signed by MGM, in addition to which she had agreed to appear in Gabriel Pascal's production of Shaw's *Androcles and the Lion*, to be made at RKO as a co-production. Simmons had six months remaining on her contract with J. Arthur Rank in England, but once she began shooting *Androcles* she discovered she now belonged to Howard Hughes. He had bought her contract without telling her. She and Granger took the case to court and won an agreement that gave Hughes the right to use her in three films for a total payment of $200,000, and her right to appear in films for other studios during the RKO agreement. They also sued Hughes for slanderous things they claim he said about them, and they received an out-of-court settlement. Simmons has never spoken well about her RKO pictures, and it must be said that none is impressive or memorable. The first, *Angel Face*, presents Simmons as a lovely psychotic and Robert Mitchum as a chauffeur whom she inveigles into her scheme to murder her step-mother (Barbara O'Neil), without his being aware of her intentions. The scheme goes awry when she also kills her beloved father (Herbert Marshall) at the same time, leading to her and the chauffeur's being charged with murder. A slick lawyer (Leon Ames) gets them off by persuading them to marry, but when the chauffeur afterwards expresses his intention to leave, she kills him and herself in a suicide plunge over a cliff in her car. Hughes brought in Otto Preminger to produce and direct this cheerless melodrama, which did fairly well at the box office.

SPLIT SECOND (1953)

By 1953 Dick Powell had tired of being merely a movie star and was looking around for a chance to step into direction. The man who gave him that chance was Howard Hughes, and the result, *Split Second*, did

Robert Newton and Linda Darnell in
Blackbeard the Pirate.

Robert Mitchum and Jean Simmons in
Angel Face.

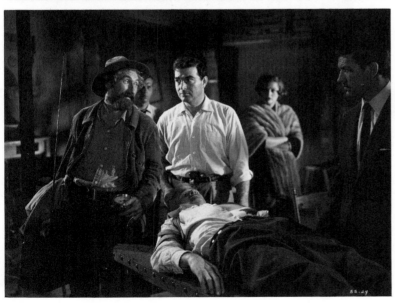

Arthur Hunnicutt, Keith Andes, Stephen
McNally, Paul Kelly, Alexis Smith and
Richard Egan in *Split Second.*

135

not cause Hughes to regret the decision. The film is a tight, suspenseful 85 minutes, centering on the predicament of a group of people held at gunpoint by a killer (Stephen McNally) in a Nevada ghost town the day before an atomic bomb is scheduled to be detonated. Among other things, what emerges is the true nature of each member of the group, with a few of the better ones surviving when they find shelter in a mine. The film revealed Powell to be a man with a fine sense of direction, especially in the tense final sequence. But Powell had to pay a price for the success; Hughes immediately signed him to direct another picture, which turned out to be *The Conqueror.*

AFFAIR WITH A STRANGER (1953)

Jean Simmons had a much more sympathetic role in her second Hughes outing, that of a model who marries a struggling playwright (Victor Mature) and helps him toward success. She loses a child by miscarriage and they adopt an orphan, but as the years go by she pays more attention to the child than the husband, who starts an affair with an actress. A gossip columnist spreads word of divorce, causing the wife to return her loving attention to the husband. Told as a series of reminiscenses by friends of the couple, it was all kept moving nicely by director Roy Rowland, and the critics commented on the fine performance and appealing image of Simmons as the loving lady.

SECOND CHANCE (1953)

Hollywood had discovered 3-D and Hughes was not about to let the discovery go unexplored. He hired Rudolph Mate, formerly a brilliant cinematographer, as director and hedged his bets by giving his top star Robert Mitchum the lead, backing him with Linda Darnell as heroine and Jack Palance as villain. The setting is South America, where Palance has been sent to kill Darnell, the ex-girlfriend of a mobster who never wants her to reveal what she knows. Prize fighter Mitchum falls in love with her and saves her. The vitally visual climax, so essential in 3-D pictures, takes place in a crippled cable car thousands of feet above a valley, with Mitchum and Palance battling to the death, although with Mitchum the obvious winner. The 3-D era did not last long in Hollywood, but *Second Chance* was one of the better entries.

DEVIL'S CANYON (1953)

There was little reason to use 3-D in this western, other than to give more perspective to the landscapes and allow horses to be ridden seemingly into the audience. Albert Werker's job as director was to keep things moving in this saga of the Arizona Territorial Prison, which houses

Victor Mature and Jean Simmons in *Affair with a Stranger*.

Linda Darnell and Jack Palance (seated at left) and Robert Mitchum in *Second Chance*.

Virginia Mayo, Stephen McNally and Jay C. Flippen in *Devil's Canyon*.

137

hundreds of outlaws, only one of whom is a woman (Virginia Mayo). She helps a tough desperado (Steven McNally) in his plan to escape because she loves him, but she turns her affections to a more decent type (Dale Robertson), an ex-lawman guilty of a revenge killing, when the brutal McNally seizes control of the prison. Mayo and Robertson receive promises of pardon for helping the warden to regain control. *Devil's Canyon* is not among the classic westerns.

THE FRENCH LINE (1954)

Perhaps feeling that his previous two 3-D pictures had not been winners, Howard Hughes now turned his attention to one he felt sure would draw attention, as it surely did. Whether Jane Russell was an innocent about the exploitation of her bust as she claims she was is open to conjecture, but once again it became the center of a storm of controversy in an otherwise conventional musical. Hughes turned over the direction to the veteran Lloyd Bacon, who had done a lot of similar lightweight musicals at Warners in the Thirties, but failed to give him much of a script or musical score to work with. The flimsy story is about an oil rich Texan (Russell) who is tired of being courted for her money and who wants a man to love her for herself. She meets such a man, a French actor (Gilbert Roland), on an ocean voyage to France, by pretending to be a working girl employed as a model by a fashion designer (Mary Mc-Carty—also a lady with a prominent bosom). When Russell and McCarty sing and dance "Any Girl from Texas," the results are, to put it mildly, riveting. But not as much as Russell's solo number, appropriately titled "Looking for Trouble," in which her statuesque torso is barely contained in a brief costume. Cameraman Harry J. Wild was obviously obeying orders in covering the Russell figure as if he were wielding a geiger counter. Seen in 3-D the results are indeed startling. Once again Hughes was battered by Hollywood's censors, who denied a production code seal. After some cutting, one was issued; the Russell solo was left intact but the whole title song was dropped, leaving nine others—none of them memorable, at least not in terms of the music.

SHE COULDN'T SAY NO (1954)

The title might well have referred to Jane Russell and *The French Line*. It referred instead to Jean Simmons as a rich girl who returns to her little home town in Arkansas (prim English accent notwithstanding) and makes gifts to the people who helped save her life when she was a child by chipping in with donations to buy hospital care. She does this anonymously until the town gets a reputation for charity and all kinds of opportunists try to take advantage of it. She then reveals her identity and settles down with the doctor (Robert Mitchum) with whom she has fallen in love. Jean Simmons clearly could not say no when she was given

Gilbert Roland and Jane Russell in *The French Line.*

this limp comedy, but she claims she would have appeared in anything to end her irksome association with Howard Hughes. This ended it. It also concluded the directing career of Lloyd Bacon—not exactly a rousing finale for some thirty years in the Hollywood trenches.

Jean Simmons and Robert Mitchum in *She Couldn't Say No.*

139

DANGEROUS MISSION (1954)

RKO's final entry in the 3-D field starred Victor Mature as an undercover police agent who follows a girl (Piper Laurie) to Glacier National Park in Montana, to which she has fled after witnessing a murder in New York. Also on her tail is a man (Vincent Price) who wants to erase her in case she ever feels like telling what she has seen. Louis King's direction was as routine as the plot, but the camera work of William Snyder and the photographic effects of Harold Wellman drew deserved comment. They captured the scope of the mountain ranges in Glacier park, a forest fire, an avalanche and a fight across the ice fields. However, by this time the public's fascination with 3-D had abated and few films used the gimmick after this one, no doubt to the relief of all film actors.

SUSAN SLEPT HERE (1954)

Dick Powell ended his long career as a movie actor with this Hollywood yarn about a top screen writer who falls in love with a delinquent teenager (Debbie Reynolds) whom a couple of his police friends bring to his home at Christmas. They reason it might be better for her to spend the holiday as his guest rather than in jail, especially as he is writing a script about problem teenagers. The plot devices range from improbable to pedestrian, but the playing of Powell and Reynolds and the direction of comedy expert Frank Tashlin makes this an enjoyable, lightweight entertainment. Powell thereafter devoted himself to the more interesting work of directing, in addition to running a successful television production company, Four Star, of which he was part owner and managing director.

UNDERWATER (1955)

Someone, perhaps even Hughes himself, decided to give Jane Russell a film in which she could be her own rather easygoing self rather than pretending to be a man-weary cynic. *Underwater*, Hughes's first film in Superscope (twice as wide as high), allowed for this kind of characterization, with Russell as the wife of an adventurous seaman (Richard Egan) who is always looking for sunken treasure. The husband finally gets a crack at a galleon teetering on a subterranean ledge, menaced by sharks and sandslides. Technicolor, a big budget and the expertise of director John Sturges made all this passingly acceptable, and many critics said it was nice to see Russell minus the vulgarity. Some sequences were filmed underwater off Hawaii, but most of the footage came from a huge studio tank at RKO. This proved to be the last time Hughes used Russell in an RKO film, but immediately afterwards he renewed his contract with her. It covered her services on six films, all of which would turn out to be loan-outs, and while Russell has reason to claim that the manner in which she was used was often questionable and distasteful, it can also be said that her Hollywood career was largely a Howard Hughes invention.

140

Piper Laurie, Victor Mature and William Bendix in *Dangerous Mission*.

Herb Virgan, Debbie Reynolds, Horace McMahon, Alvy Moore and Dick Powell in *Susan Slept Here*.

Richard Egan and Jane Russell in *Underwater*.

141

SON OF SINBAD (1955)

Believe it or not, this Arabian Nights absurdity was made for purposes other than merely to draw customers—which it easily did since it was nothing more than a parade of lovely, scantily dressed young ladies pretending to be harem slaves of Old Bagdad. All through his years at RKO, Hughes had continually placed girls under contract, some of them beauty contest winners, most of them aspiring actresses who were promised lessons in their craft and development of their careers. Gina Lollobrigida, for example, was brought over from Italy, but after months of being couped up in a hotel and never getting to the studio this fiery actress stormed out of her plush prison and went home. The French ballet star Jeanmarie was brought to Hollywood by Hughes, along with her entire ballet troupe, but the only work she did was in Goldwyn's *Hans Christian Andersen*. Perhaps as many as a hundred others held Hughes contracts, contracts which promised them at least one part in a film. *Son of Sinbad* was the clearing house for these promises. Ted Tetzlaff was assigned as director and script writers Aubrey Wisberg and Jack Pollexfen were ordered to whip up a story. Dale Robertson was given the role of Sinbad junior, and Vincent Price, barely able to keep tongue in cheek, was required to play poet Omar Khayyam. The plot had something to do with Sinbad's saving Bagdad from the ambitions of Tamerlane, not that it mattered. Hughes was able to hereby fulfill his contractual obligations to a horde of pretty ladies. They may have been only extras in a harem but they would have no legals legs on which to stand if they brought suit. *Son of Sinbad* and *Underwater* were the only two Hughes films to appear in 1955. RKO released twelve other pictures that year but they were all co-productions. It was the studio's most meager year in terms of product, and it did not auger well.

THE CONQUEROR (1956)

Not long after Hughes sold his interests in RKO and ceased to be a movie mogul, he bought back two of the films in which he had invested his time and interest. Both starred his friend John Wayne. They were *The Conqueror* and *Jet Pilot*, and Hughes shelled out millions to acquire total ownership. It is unlikely that he recouped more than a fraction of the price, especially with the latter picture. *The Conqueror* is generally regarded as the most ludicrous of Wayne's major films and as such he could blame no one but himself. He had contracted to make one more film for RKO and as a powerhouse box office attraction he could call his shots. Also contracted for one more film was director Dick Powell, who was astonished when Wayne told him he wanted to play the part of Mongol emperor Genghis Khan. Said Powell, "At first I was surprised. Wayne as the barbarous Genghis Khan? I asked him if he was serious and he said he was. I was unprepared for the situation but John was insistent. Who was I to turn down Wayne?"

142

Lili St. Cyr and Dale Robertson in *Son of Sinbad.*

Hughes made Powell the producer as well as director and gave him a budget of six million dollars. It would be not only the final film made by Hughes but his most expensive. Locations were chosen near the town of St. George, amid the awesome scenery of southwest Utah, and local

John Wayne and Ted de Corsia in *The Conqueror.*

143

Indians were hired as horse-riding Mongol and Tartar tribesmen. Hughes paid for the state to build roads to the location and Powell found himself in command of a company of five hundred cast and crew. With another actor in the lead the film might have worked, but with Wayne it was merely another western, albeit one with exotic costumes. As spectacle *The Conqueror* is sometimes visually brilliant, with hordes of ferocious tribesmen galloping over the landscape. It becomes ridiculous when Wayne addresses the fiery Bortai (Susan Hayward), the daughter of the Tartar king, with lines like, "I shall keep you, Bortai. In response to my passion, your hatred will kindle into love."

The plot in brief: Bortai is captured by Genghis Khan, who becomes smitten with her beauty and defiance. She escapes, but in following her Genghis is captured and tortured by her brutal father; this causes her to sympathize with the equally brutal Genghis, and with growing feelings of love she sets him free, leading to an eventual defeat of the Tartars by Genghis, and Bortai as his bride.

With its massive publicity campaign *The Conqueror* received wide bookings and made back most of its production costs, but not enough to cover the publicity and the cost of scores of prints. The only person who really loved the picture was Howard Hughes, who eventually bought up all the prints and withdrew the film. He apparently watched it hundreds of times. It was not seen again until 1974, when Paramount secured distribution rights and issued it on a double bill with *Jet Pilot*, for what proved to be a limited run.

JET PILOT (1957)

Of all Hughes's failures at RKO nothing was more conspicuous or sadder than *Jet Pilot*. Like David O. Selznick, who could never top his own *Gone With the Wind*, Hughes wanted to make something that would at least equal *Hell's Angels*. The most obvious way to do it was to make a modern aerial epic, something that would be to the jet age what the other film was to First World War aviation. Production began in December of 1949, with John Wayne as the obvious choice for the hero, a U.S. Army Air Corp colonel. For reasons best known to himself, Hughes borrowed the pretty but not very experienced Janet Leigh to play a Russian jet pilot.

Jules Furthman invented a far-fetched screenplay, which Hughes liked so much he made Furthman his producer. The job of director was given to an unlikely choice, the esthetic Josef von Sternberg, best remembered for his handling of the early Marlene Dietrich pictures. Von Sternberg may have needed the job, but he bridled under Hughes. After he left, a lot of footage was re-shot by Nicholas Ray, who claims that as much as half the material viewable in *Jet Pilot* is actually his.

The story has Wayne as the commander of an air base in Alaska

Janet Leigh and John Wayne in *Jet Pilot*.

and the man put in charge of a Soviet pilot (Janet Leigh) who lands at the base and declares herself a defector. He takes her to Washington where he wines and dines her as well as discusses aviation. He marries her, but once his bosses convince him she is really a Soviet spy, he enters into a counter-espionage plot and escapes to Russia with her. There she sees that her side are really the villains and that she loves her American colonel, so they steal a jet plane and fly back to America.

Had Hughes released the film as soon as it was initially completed he may have gotten by with a minor success, but this was his baby and he was a perfectionist. Ironically, what defeated Hughes the film maker was the rapidly changing and developing state of affairs in his other industry—aviation. He constantly sought aerial footage from his extensive contacts in the Air Force and industry, but as soon as it was edited it was made obsolete by new developments in aircraft. He wanted it to be the last word in movies about jet aviation, but this caused delay after delay—over an astonishing eight-year period.

When finally released in September of 1957, all 112 minutes of it, uninformed viewers were surprised to find John Wayne looking far younger than in his last two pictures, *The Searchers* and *The Wings of Eagles*. Every critic pounced on the ludicrous story lines, and several said the aerial footage was not all that remarkable. The estimable critic of *The New York Times*, Bosley Crowther, put his finger on the problem: "Wars have been fought and airplane designs have been improved since *Jet Pilot* went before the cameras in 1949 ... and a good many better motion pictures about jet pilots have gone over the dam ... ."

Jet Pilot was the last film ever to bear the opening credit line, "Howard Hughes Presents."

It may look like the set of a science-fiction film but it is actually the flightdeck of Howard Hughes' massive flying boat, "The Spruce Goose." This was the day Hughes, looking over the shoulder of his flight engineer, took the plane on its one and only flight—November 2, 1947, a flight of only a minute or so over the waters of Long Beach Harbor.

Hollywood Afterlife

Pauline

Howard Hughes no doubt breathed an enormous sigh of relief on July 19, 1955, when the sale of his interests in RKO was finalized. He had not been a success as the mastermind and commanding officer of a motion picture studio, although he could take a small amount of comfort in reflecting that none of the other movie moguls had done much better during the same period. The old Hollywood, the Hollywood of massive movie factories dominating the film world and making profits almost automatically, had been crumbling for some time. The block bookings on theatre circuits controlled by the studios had gone, the star system had passed, and by 1955 it was obvious that the only way to beat the enemy, television, was to join it. Nothing made that more obvious than the sale of RKO, a film production company, to Desilu, a TV company, two years later. MGM, Warners, Paramount and Universal were not going to allow themselves to suffer the same fate.

Hughes's years as the leader of RKO cannot truly be described as anything less than disastrous. RKO had suffered all kinds of ups and downs in its history, but from 1948 to 1955 it did not need an absentee landlord, one who kept his offices someplace other than at the studio and who could only be reached, if at all, by strange arrangements with messengers and delayed communications. In the nervous, febrile world of film making, decisions need to be immediate, egos need to be understood, insecure talents need to be subtly supported, and balance

Tommy Lee Jones in the television film *The Amazing Howard Hughes*, (top) as Hughes at the time of piloting "The Spruce Goose," and in his last, hermetic years.

147

needs to be brought to bear in an ever-teetering business. Hughes was about as wrong for the job as can be imagined.

During Hughes's RKO years his interests in his other enterprises grew tremendously, especially in aviation. How much of this growth in his wealth is directly attributable to his own efforts is debatable, but it was after leaving the picture business that the millionaire became a billionaire. In addition to his industrial activities during the RKO years, he also took a great step forward, at least in his own thinking, by setting up the Howard Hughes Medical Institute in Florida. More of a hypochondriac than ever, and truly dedicated to the fight against germs and disease, he wanted his institute to inherit most of his wealth and accomplish something monumentally good in his name.

Although free from the onerous job of managing a film studio, Hughes did occasionally think about making movies again, but none of his ideas came to fruition. His retreat from RKO also coincided with a winding down of his Hollywood social life. He had acquired a considerable reputation as a ladies' man, with almost all the ladies being involved with the movies. The list is long and impressive. It is perhaps easier to draw up a list of famous actresses who were not dated by Hughes than of those who were. One of his most sustained affairs in the late Thirties was with the patrician Katharine Hepburn, and how serious it was will never be known since Hepburn remains adamant about discussing her private life—a characteristic she shared with Hughes. She also shared his passion for golf and flying, which clearly gave her the edge on most of his dates. But finally, since she had no interest in marrying him, they came to an amicable parting.

A prime subject for the gossip columnists, Hughes sometimes found himself reputedly engaged to women he had never even met. One of them was Olivia de Havilland, whom he called to apologize and then asked for a date. They were seen together on a number of occasions and rumors of marriage began to emerge, but Hughes squelched them by announcing that he had no intention of marrying again until he was fifty. De Havilland says, "I remember Howard with gratitude. I'm also grateful we did not marry. Marriage would have been unfortunate."

Women, with the exception of Terry Moore, have been reluctant to discuss Hughes on the intimate level. He apparently never socialized with those actresses whom he had under important contracts. Jane Russell has often said that in her opinion he was such a shy man that she could not imagine him being aggressive or forceful with women. Be that as it may, Hughes was seen in the company of Linda Darnell, Lana Turner, Yvonne DeCarlo, Elizabeth Taylor, Mitzi Gaynor and Ava Gardner. All of them were subjected to surveillance during their periods of being his girl friends; he wanted them checked out for competition and also for medical reasons. Being spied upon and tailed no doubt cooled the ardor of most of them. Ava Gardner became so incensed by Hughes's strange ways that she reportedly hit him over the head with a heavy ashtray and knocked him out.

In the early Thirties Hughes frequently dated Ginger Rogers, and in the years before he became reclusive they danced together in nightclubs. Recalls Rogers, "Howard was a very good dancer—he loved to dance. He was an all-round brilliant fellow." She adds, "The sad part is that he was a loner. And loners are very unhappy people." While this is undoubtably true, it is also obvious that Hughes made life more difficult for himself by his odd habits, one of the oddest of which was his reluctance to carry money. Terry Moore tells of being picked up by him in his plain, indistinct Chevrolet—the days of his driving fast sports cars were long gone—and dressed in plain, indistinct clothes, and being personally flown by Hughes from Los Angeles to the Grand Canyon. She naturally expected to be treated to a meal, but the only money they had between them was one dollar in her own pockets, which they spent on sandwiches and then flew back to Los Angeles.

Terry Moore also claims to have been married to Hughes. The ceremony allegedly took place on a yacht cruising the Mexican coast in 1949, but whatever written evidence of that marriage there may have been has never been found. In her book *The Beauty and the Billionaire*, Moore cites Hughes as the best lover she ever had, and paints a picture of him as a man of strong sexuality. In her pages he appears to be a virtual satyr, as well as a man chronically unable to be faithful. He also, by this account, made more than one date at a time and sped back and forth between women during a single evening. There is no evidence of Hughes's having sired any children, but Moore says that she gave birth to a child by him in Munich in 1951, but that the baby was born prematurely and died within hours. Her claim on the marriage was strong enough, or persistent enough, for the Hughes estate to make a 1983 settlement with her for an unstated amount. Says Moore, "I can live off the interest for the rest of my life."

Howard Hughes's marriage to Jean Peters is well documented. He met her not long after her arrival in Hollywood—as a beauty contest winner from Ohio—when she was placed under contract to 20th Century-Fox and given as her first role the lead opposite Tyrone Power in *Captain from Castile*. Filmed in 1946, when Peters was twenty, this swashbuckling epic was the kind of glittering debut seldom awarded newcomers, and it launched her on a string of successes. Peters was not a girl attracted to the bright lights of Hollywood social life, and she chose to live quietly. Once Hughes became smitten with her and offered to take her wherever she wished he was probably greatly relieved to find she preferred out-of-the-way places where neither of them would be recognized. But however she might have felt about Hughes, she decided to marry another man, Stuart W. Cramer, in May of 1954.

The Peters-Cramer marriage was a failure and they separated after a year, at which time Hughes eagerly resumed his courtship of the girl he now realized he loved. He married her on January 12, 1957, in a small ceremony in Tonopah, Nevada, and with no press coverage. Hughes had sold his Los Angeles house in 1945 because he did not want to be taxed as a California resident (one of the many ploys in his constant battles with taxation), and he and his bride first lived in a bungalow on the grounds

149

Jean Peters, as she appeared with
Richard Todd in *A Man Called Peter*
(1955), the film with which she ended
her movie career in favor of becoming
Mrs. Howard Hughes.

of the Beverly Hills Hotel. This manner of living was not to the tastes of Mrs. Hughes, so he then rented a large home in Bel-Air, the ritziest and quietest area of Los Angeles. The house was deliberately inaccessible and well guarded by a team of resident employees.

The intimate details of his marriage with Jean Peters are not likely to be known, since she has steadfastly refused to talk about these years of her life or to accept the many offers she has received from publishers. It can only be assumed that it was not a conventional marriage; they appear to have occupied separate quarters, and people employed by them at the time have told of Peters dropping by her husband's dark, secluded bedroom at appointed times. Any assumptions beyond this are unwise. But she did end her film career with the marriage, her last film being *A Man Called Peter* in 1955, and she behaved with dignity at all times.

Whatever his failures in trying to run a movie studio, there was much success for Hughes in aviation. In February of 1956 he ordered thirty-three Boeing 707 jet airliners for TWA, while Hughes Aircraft continued to build for the military. But the strain of all these enterprises caught up with him in the middle of 1958, when he suffered his second nervous breakdown. TWA developed into a real problem for Hughes, with much contention among the owners, and he was compelled to sell his shares in 1966 for $546 million. In November of that year, tired of living in California with all its tax problems, he decided to take up residence in Nevada, where the tax laws were more liberal and where he was intrigued by the idea of building more businesses. In the Spring of 1967 Hughes acquired control of the Desert Inn and Casino in Las Vegas, making it his home and the headquarters of his Nevada enterprises. Among other things he bought Air West in 1970, but it was also the year he lost out on his marriage. Jean Peters announced divorce proceedings, which became final a year later.

The divorce was uncontested and Hughes made no adverse comments about his ex-wife. All efforts to get any statements from Peters proved a failure, leading people to assume that her settlement with him possibly prohibited comment. There appear to be no grounds for this assumption. In 1971 Peters signed a new agreement with Hughes which provided her with an annual $70,000 for twenty years, and there was nothing in the agreement stipulating her not to discuss Hughes. The discretion has been of her own choosing.

After divorcing Jean Peters, Hughes was never again connected with any famous actresses. Indeed, his personal life after 1971 was either secretive or barely existent. The last dozen or so years in the life of Howard Hughes appear to involve only business and legal dealings, and it was a period of rapid financial gain. In 1970 he acquired a number of other holdings in the state of Nevada, but it was in November of that year that he left that state and moved into the Britannia Beach Hotel on Paradise Island in the Bahamas. Hughes would never return to the United States—the last six years were those of an itinerant exile, moving from one luxurious hotel to another with his staff and business entourage.

Hughes's business dealings became more and more complex and involved ceaseless legal battles. By leaving America he was at least able to avoid process servers, but the hassles and the travels could not have done much to improve his failing health. In February of 1972 he moved to The Intercontinental Hotel in Managua, Nicaragua, a month later to the Bayshore Inn in Vancouver, British Columbia, for six months, and then back to Managua. In December of that year he moved to The Inn on the Park in London and stayed there for two years. This was followed by a move to The Xanadu Princess Hotel, Freeport, in the Bahamas, until February of 1976, when he made the final move to Acapulco. There is no reason to believe that Hughes enjoyed any of these luxurious accommodations and locations because in most of them he lived a totally secluded life behind drawn curtains.

Hughes made a surprising transaction in 1972 when he sold Hughes Tool Company, which had been his fairy godmother since the death of his father. He, or his advisers, considered it no longer necessary, and it was sold for $150 million. After he died the assets of his Summa Corporation, under which all his businesses were governed, were valued at two billion dollars. These assets were represented by land holdings in Nevada and California, hotels, Hughes Airwest, a television station, various mining concerns, and, most of all, Hughes Aircraft Company. This, by now a major defense contractor producing weapons and space-age technology, accounted for half the assets. Since 1954 it had been wholly owned by the Howard Hughes Medical Institute, with Hughes its only trustee.

Among the minor assets was a company called Hughes Productions, which leased his films and proved that he had never completely dropped out of the motion picture business. He also never lost his fascination with the movies. He viewed them every day and it is possible that he saw just about every film made in Hollywood. As a young producer he had projectionists on call at all times, although the hours when he usually watched movies were those in the middle of the night. In every home and in every hotel suite he had a projector, with an endless supply of 16 mm prints, and this went on right up until the move to Acapulco. Movies and TV seem to have been his only entertainment.

One film in which Hughes had particular interest was *The Carpetbaggers*, which Paramount released in 1964. His interest was legal. Producer Joseph L. Levine bought the rights to the Harold Robbins novel, which had obviously been inspired by the Hughes story, since the leading character, Jonas Cord, Jr., was a man who was greatly successful in aviation and movies, and had a strong liking for women. The astute Robbins had carefully structured his parallels and surrounded them with copious fiction, so as not to invite a law suit. But Hughes felt sensitive about all this being put on the screen and demanded that Paramount allow his lawyers to see the film before it was released. Paramount, not about to tackle a man who still carried clout in Hollywood, complied.

George Peppard as Jonas Cord, Jr., in *The Carpetbaggers* (1964), a characterization obviously inspired by Howard Hughes. With Peppard are Charles Lane, Elizabeth Ashley and Arthur Franz.

Hughes's chief attorney, Greg Bautzer, a prominent name in the film community, afterwards said with some disgust, "Any day in the life of Howard Hughes is more exciting than that whole mucking film." No action of any kind was taken by Hughes, and Paramount and Levine proceeded to make a great profit. George Peppard's portrayal of the reckless, unscrupulous, unkind young Cord advanced his film career, but there was little about the projected image that bore much similarity to the quiet, reclusive man Robert Mitchum so aptly tagged "The Phantom."

The Carpetbaggers also provided Carroll Baker with a career advancement, playing a Jean Harlow-type of actress named Rina Marlowe. In Robbins's novel she is the sexy young wife of Cord senior, young enough to be his daughter, and after he dies of a sudden heart attack she is romanced by Cord junior, who turns her into a movie star. This piece of invention was nothing of concern to Hughes or his lawyers, but they were upset when Joseph L. Levine announced that he was going to star Baker in a movie about Jean Harlow. Levine acquired the rights to Irving Shulman's best selling, spicy biography, *Harlow*, and Hughes had cause to wonder how he might be portrayed in the film. The fact that *Hell's Angels* made Harlow a star could hardly be overlooked.

Movie biographies can never be regarded as accurate documents. In the interests of entertainment the facts tend to be regarded as points of departure rather than basis, and this is especially true in the films Hollywood has made about its own people. *Harlow* gave neither Hughes nor the public reason to believe otherwise. In this glossy, and not very

153

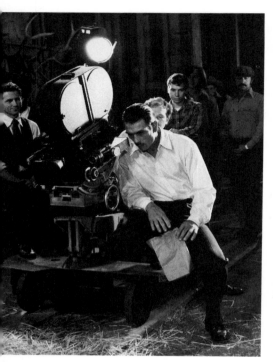

Tommy Lee Jones and a recreation of Hughes directing *The Outlaw.*

successful, account of the tragic Harlow's life, Leslie Nielsen plays a film producer named Richard Manley, who gives Harlow her big chance and expects sexual favors in return. He invites her to his plush, bachelor bedroom and tries to seduce her, but she knees him in the groin and leaves. Since Harlow herself went on record as saying that Hughes never so much as touched her, there was no reason for a libel suit. Just before Levine brought out his version, producer Bill Sargent turned out a cheap, videotape *Harlow* starring Carol Lynley, but the film made little impact. The nearest it came to Hughes was a scene showing the making of *Hell's Angel,* with the gentlemanly English actor John Williams playing the director. It seems nearer to James Whale than Hughes, and certainly nothing for the Hughes lawyers to give a second thought.

The first actual depiction of Hughes on the screen came in April of 1977, exactly a year after his death, when Roger Gimbell Productions aired their telefilm *The Amazing Howard Hughes,* starring Tommy Lee Jones in the title role. The two-part, four-hour picture was a fairly straightforward accounting of Hughes's life, with Jones giving a strong but not arresting characterization. The fault was not that of the actor but more probably of the scripting and direction in trying to make a serious study of a shy, retiring eccentric. The result was somewhat dulling. John Gay's script was based on the book, *Howard, The Amazing Mr. Hughes,* by Noah Dietrich and Bob Thomas. Dietrich's intimate association up until the day he was fired, May 12, 1957, cannot be questioned, but since the film dealt at length with Hughes's adventures after that date it must be assumed that Dietrich and his collaborator fell back on second-hand accounts. There is also the factor of bitterness on the part of Dietrich, which is understandable in view of the summary manner in which he was dismissed after almost thirty-five years of service—and dismissed without severance pay or pension.

After his death the Hughes estate was swamped with claims on his will, especially when it became apparent that the legality of the estate was somewhat in confusion due to Hughes's either not having left clearly spelled out instructions as to the disposition of his assets and interests, or having had his instructions altered or interfered with. In the last year or so of his life Hughes was still putting his signature to business and legal papers, but with no one contesting his competence to do so. His physical health was pitiful during that period, and with his addiction to codeine it becomes doubtful if all his decisions were made with a clear mind. In September of 1975 a group of his top aides and executives were able to receive lifetime employment contracts from him. Whether or not this was a rational decision on his part is pure conjecture.

Something like six hundred claims were levied against the Hughes will, with almost all of them proven false. The most bizarre concerned a young Utah gas station attendant named Melvin Dummar. He claimed that Hughes willed him $156 million dollars and as evidence he produced a will which had been mysteriously sent to him. The three-page will was presumably written by Hughes by hand and left at the Morman Church headquarters in Salt Lake City. Dated April 17, 1968, it

Melvin and Howard, with Paul Le Mat as Melvin.

contained a dozen misspelled words and grammatical errors the educated Hughes would not likely have made, and Dummar's claim was thrown out of court. The case created a great deal of attention and led to among other things a 1980 Universal movie titled *Melvin and Howard*, with Paul Le Mat as the claimant and Jason Robards as Hughes.

Melvin and Howard pleased the movie critics but drew little reaction from the public. Perhaps they had heard too much about it from the media, or perhaps they felt it was too silly to attend. If so, the judgment is somewhat harsh. It is an interesting film, and Bo Goldman's screenplay gives a sympathetic account of both characters. Robards as Hughes is seen for only ten minutes of screentime, mostly in the first reel and then a little at the end. The film begins with a wild old man riding a motorcycle around the partly moonlit Nevada desert at night. He falls off and hurts himself, and sometime later he is spotted lying on the side of a road by Melvin, who hesitatingly picks up the strange, shabby old man with thin, matted white hair, sickly pale complexion and furtive eyes. Melvin tries to amuse the old man with some of his own songs—he wants to be a song writer—but the old man would rather sing "Bye, Bye Blackbird" as they make their way to Las Vegas. Melvin lets him off at the Sands Hotel, where the old man tells the doubtful Melvin he lives. He also tells him his name and borrows twenty-five cents. Years pass, Howard Hughes dies ... and a will turns up at Melvin's gas station. Thus *Melvin and Howard*, a film best remembered for Robard's performance as a weird and wonderful old man plucked from the desert night—and most probably from someone's overheated imagination.

Howard Hughes will no doubt emerge again in film form in the years to come but, as is always the case in trying to depict larger-than-

Jason Robards, Jr., as Howard Hughes in *Melvin and Howard.*

life historical characters, the results will probably fail, because such men make little sense in novels and movies. They belong only in real life, with its total lack of logic, rationale or rules. In fiction it makes no sense to tell of a young man who persuades a court that he is competent to inherit a valuable business at nineteen, runs his own affairs, goes to Hollywood and makes movies, designs airplanes, breaks speed records, flies around the world, romances dozens of the world's most beautiful women, builds the biggest airplane ever known, buys and runs airlines, owns an aircraft company that builds equipment to conquer space, turns into a total recluse and leaves an estate worth two billion dollars. Such men, of course, do not really exist. Except in one instance.

Since this book has focussed on Howard Hughes's activities in the area of motion pictures, the last words rightly belong to someone who also made his mark in that area—writer-producer Dore Schary. They had nothing in common either as men or as artists; Hughes had caused Schary to leave RKO in a state of anger, and yet Hughes would sometimes turn to this very dissimilar man and ask for advice, and also tell him he would do anything to help him if only Schary would ask. When Schary heard that Hughes had died in the air while being flown from Acapulco to Houston, he said, "I am positive that if he had had a choice and could have elected the way he wanted to die, he would have chosen to be in an airplane in flight. I am glad that the wish was granted to him."

Dore Schary also said something about Howard Hughes that makes any further comment redundant: "In spite of his reclusive and odd nature, there is no gainsaying the fact that he was a heroic, strange and mystical figure who was blessed with courage and cursed with loneliness."

Index